GW00691459

Memory Rings the Bells

Previous publications,

Kaleidoscope of Living Thoughts.
I'm Jane.

Memory Rings
The Bells

Presented by Betty and Ken Collins

Regency Press (London & New York) Ltd.
125 High Holborn, London WC1V 6QA

ISBN 0 7212 0881 9

Printed and bound in Great Britain by
Buckland Press Ltd., Dover, Kent.

CONTENTS

PROLOGUE

I wanted to write a dedication for this book, and an introduction, so that the reader has some idea of the contents and my appreciation for the help I have received in the making of it.

I find these things so interwoven, so much a part of each other, that I cannot separate them. I shall therefore let them stay together where they belong, and present them to you as one, the "prologue".

There have been so many kindly people who are important to my life and the production of this book, that a comprehensive list would be too long and I would run the risk of overlooking someone's name who should be included. Therefore, whilst dedicating "Memory Rings The Bells" to all who have played their part, I will mention just the few who for one reason or another seem to have played leading roles at particular times – some for a lifetime, some a brief encounter.

To begin at the beginning then – I must start with my wonderful father and mother and my mother's parents (the grass roots of my life). Then there is my cousin Winnie and her husband Wally – I owe them both so much. My friend James Cooper (Jimmie, a lesson himself in dedication), and a working colleague Freddie Magin, who set me on the spiritual path. There is also my mother's younger brother (my favourite uncle), and his patient wife (a second mother). Readers may be interested to know that this uncle is the artist who is responsible for the drawings in this and our two previous books – the related facts are given elsewhere in this book. All these friends and relations are now in Spirit, they helped me in earthly life and assist me still.

The story of how the title and this book came into being is partly given here and also under another heading "The Message of the Bells". All the memories I have recorded here are fact, the observations that they ignite are mostly inspired spirit writing, usually at great speed and in a different handwriting to that used for recording the incidents gleaned from my memory. Other chapters were received in trance from our own Communicator and are offered with explanatory notes where necessary.

With a considerable amount of material lying idle in folders for want of a purpose, we were mindful of a prediction from the Guide of international medium Hilda Martin in 1984, that we would be publishing a third book – which seemed highly unlikely at the time – but her Guide seemed quite certain.

It was February 1987 when one of my own Guides made one of her rare communications, and with the following words told us that we could now begin the book: . . . "Now we want you to start another (book) . . . it should be a month by month account of memories, poems, articles, drawings, hymns for which we will try to give the music . . . it will be a pot-pourri of thought on many different levels of thinking and knowledge, and will therefore help and give pleasure to a great many people".

And so it was with a certain amount of trepidation we set out on the adventure of "Memory Rings The Bells", prompted and guided at every turn by spirit friends, guides and helpers. My gratitude is due to all of them and the many people who have been part of my experience of life and therefore part of this book. I have learnt much and been spared a great deal because of each one, in special individual ways.

Special thanks are due to my friend Dorothy Middleton for her patient deciphering, typing and advice, and last but by no means least, the kindly patient help of Ken, without whose checking abilities, encouragement and support, none of it could have happened, for he provided the power whilst I contribute my memory and limited know-how.

To each and every one my heartfelt thanks. I only hope that my own contributions are worthy of their efforts, and that this book will add its quota of help to those who need it in any way whatsoever. If it succeeds in this, then the efforts of us all will be worthy of its purpose. Different parts of the book will appeal to different people, perhaps according to their need or their understanding. We feel confident that anyone who makes the time and effort to read it through, will find something rewarding for them, maybe a little comfort, some encouragement, perhaps a flash of recognition, or even just a smile.

I leave it now in the hands of our readers to assess the contents for themselves, and perhaps find that for them also, "Memory Rings The Bells".

WHEN MEMORY RINGS THE BELLS

When memory rings the bells of truth
To bring a message loud and clear,
Or gently chimes a simple proof
That older moments re-appear,
Of Spirit's power to guide and soothe
As memory rings the bells.

As our memories search the heights
And depths, of all our earthly lives,
We find small gems and pure delights,
As resurrecting thought revives
The fading sounds, forgotten sights
As memory rings the bells.

We know God's ever loving power,
And the guidance that He gives,
We see His craftsmanship in flower
With everything that lives
And beauty in each passing hour,
While memory rings the bells.

At last life's many mysteries
Stand shiningly revealed,
Now we can see life's histories,
For evermore unsealed
By truth of Spirit's purposes
When memory rings the bells.

JANUARY GARDEN

Drab and brown, but sometimes white
Crispy frost for our delight.
I did not know grass blades could be
Such fine and perfect filigree.

Branches bare on sleeping trees,
So stark and black they seem to be.
I did not know that twigged and branched,
The dark grey sky could be enhanced.

The muddy patches, scuffed up grass,
Cold winds and rain all come to pass.
I did not know how red and round
A robin is, on winter's ground.

Dead brown heads of last year flowers
Give memories of sunnier hours.
I did not know that winter's jasmin
Would cascade now, in gold profusion.

Driving snow or freezing sleet,
Make us welcome fireside heat.
I did not know the garden's charm
From cosy window, snug and warm.

★ ★ ★ ★ ★

WORDS

It is an interesting speculation to consider the number of words spoken in the world each day, and the enormous number of printed words that rest upon the bookshelves of libraries and homes. Obviously they are of primary importance to us all, and yet we often give little thought to the effects they have on others.

As this book is itself adding to that vast accumulation, our Communicator, in 1985, thought fit to deliver the following reminder on their use. It seems an appropriate way to begin the telling of memories that serve to ring some bells.

Let us reflect for a few moments on the use of words. Words can be the poetry of life. Entwined with the flowers of loving truth, they are the perfect gift to those in need of upliftment in sorrow, or add to the happiness of the joyful. Words can heal those that are sick in body, mind or soul and so fulfil their greatest purpose. Use words in these ways to add to the love and peace of your world.

But words can also be used as barbs of cruelty, deceit and hate, bringing to your earth unhappiness, disruption and war.

Ensure that words are used aright. Propelled by happy thoughts and loving peace, they will bring these things to all around you. If each and everyone will do their part, then peace and love can filter into the darkest corners of your world, and bring to it the shining light of God.

HEALING WORDS

The blessing of a healing word,
Is Spirits' healing power.
When words of peace and love are heard,
The healing is in flower.

When healing words flow rich and free
To take away all gloom,
They gather so that all may see
God's garden in full bloom.

★ ★ ★ ★ ★

THE MESSAGE OF THE BELLS

When I was very small indeed, we were the proud owners of a
gramophone in an oak case, which you wound up, inserted a steel
needle in the sound head and very gently placed it upon the revolving
record. One of my father's favourites was a piece called "Bells Across
The Meadow" which seemed to stem from his own boyhood memory
of cylinder records that were one of the wonders of that period. The
bells and meadows are one of my clearest memories of young
childhood, and looking back, I suspect that it was the earliest portent of
what was to come very much later.

Whilst sitting quietly in meditation one morning in 1988, I heard a
lady's gentle voice quite clearly – "Memory rings the bells" she said. I
repeated it so that my husband Ken would register it in his own mind –

a habit we both use to prevent something useful being lost. Afterwards I wrote it down and relegated it to a folder of other such snippets, both long and short. It didn't mean anything at the time, but some months later whilst writing for this our third book, I heard the voice again, repeating the same words – the penny suddenly dropped – it was the title of the book, but a strange one I thought at first as I pondered on the words.

The more I thought about it, the more I realised how apt it was, for not only did it fit in with much that had already been written, but it was also in keeping with the theme of the book itself. Years ago, people were much more conscious of the message of the bells, and the rural population in particular would know by the way the village church bells were rung, exactly what was going on. The different 'changes' rang out across the meadows, to call the people to service, to tell of a wedding or funeral, and these three are still in common usage today. Even though many modern folk may not be able to interpret the messages in those ringing tones, they still give pleasure and perhaps comfort, especially in rural communities, where memories are handed down like folk lore.

During the Second World War, our church bells were silenced and their use confined to warning of invasion, or as a message of victory. Happily they were only required for celebration. Other bells have traditionally been used for many purposes. The town crier rang his bell to call attention to the information he would then cry out. On ships they clanged to change the Watches, in sitting rooms to call the parlour maid, in schools to assemble the pupils, and Muffin Men rang them to tell prospective muffin eaters that they were on their way. While firemen rang their bell to clear the streets ahead of the fire engine as it rushed to urgent rescue, and newsboys on bikes rang their bicycle bells to warn of their hurried, wobbly approach. All these bells and many more fulfilled the task of conveying a message of some kind.

Here in this book my own memories have rung the bells, so that they can each bring a message, perhaps from some far off incident or maybe a more recent experience – unimportant in itself, but acquiring greater value with time and retrospect. The exercise has created patterns that demonstrate how simple thoughts and actions can have far reaching results. In delving into my personal box of memories, I have been able to retrieve some of the best and nicest treasures and often the simplest, to bring their own particular messages, perhaps of hope or enlightenment, maybe to point a different line of thought or action, or create a better understanding of another point of view, or perhaps quite simply to uplift and bring a smile.

The message of the bells reminds us too, that all our thoughts, words and actions are capable of such resurrection, the bad as well as the good, and a lesson can be learnt from all of them. This realisation must surely be an encouragement to create only the best memories for ourselves or others to use, so that we can add in our own small way to the sum total of good and kindness in the world. This seems to be the purpose of this book, planned and guided by Spirit from my earliest years.

By hindsight, I see the pattern that has unfolded before my very eyes and ears, little thinking of such a use for it as this. It has not been an easy task to begin to write when memory rang a bell, and find each ringing drifting into some unconsidered philosophical line of thought. Neither has it been simple to amalgamate the more recent communications with the older ones to make a balanced, flowing whole. Without the guidance of my Spirit friends it would never have been accomplished. But if every reader finds herein something helpful to his or her own living, the effort will have been well rewarded. Just as the bells of long ago rang out across the meadows to tell their message loud and clear, so these memories of mine, will I hope ring a bell or two for you and be music to your ears.

From the clutter of my memory box, or if you like, the ragbag of my life, these few pieces of material have emerged to create a patchwork picture that will find its niche somewhere, give help where help is needed and raise a smile to brighten someone's way. It must be so, because it is the work of Spirit and it has been my privilege to provide the pen and paper, or sometimes to sit in trance while their message was recorded.

As I look out of our window to the green patchwork of fields, and hear the message of the bells from a distant church tower, I realise I have come full circle – I am back to the "Bells Across The Meadow" of my childhood, where it all began.

A PRAYER

Dear Father God, please lend to me, the wisdom of Thy peace, that I may use it well, and by passing it to others, I may return the loan and pay my debt to Thee.

Help me share the gifts I have received, that those in need around me may know the strength of Thy own love for us. Please grant to me dear Father, a small portion of Thy strength, that through my heart, my mind and body, I may help those in need around me, and by my own administrations to them, give my thanks to Thee.

The following hymn was found scribbled in a rather scrawly handwriting, having obviously been written with two different pens on two scraps of paper. It can be sung to a 7878D metre, the tunes Beecher, Austria, What a Friend and Love Divine, (the latter played twice for each verse).

THE JOY OF SINGING

Oh the happy joy of living
With our Father's holy love,
How we love the joy of singing
With His choirs from above.
Oh the joy of every blessing
Reaching out to every heart,
May we feel that love caressing
Bidding earthly fear depart.

Help us Lord to ever seek Thee
In our daily working lives,
Help us share our joy so freely,
Cast away another's sighs.
Thank you Father for your giving
To Thy children here on earth,
Help us use the joy of singing
Giving happiness rebirth.

★ ★ ★ ★ ★

SYMBOLISM

Those dedicated souls that come to us from the world of Spirit in order that we may benefit from their teaching and philosophy, frequently use symbolism as a method of helping us to understand. By equating the messages they bring to circumstances that are familiar to us on the earthplane, they can overcome many problems they experience in linking the two worlds, and help us to overcome our own earthplane difficulties in understanding them. Here are two examples of their use of symbolic teaching.

It is an interesting thought that we teach our small children here on earth by means of pictures, our own drawings perhaps, or by helping the child to draw. Presumably we, with our limited spiritual knowledge, are as children to those of much greater knowledge in the spirit world, and can be taught effectively in the same way.

It is worth remembering that these very knowledgeable guides have themselves passed through the school of earthplane learning at some time or other, and so will know the best way of helping us from their own personal experience. The fact that they choose to come to us with the superior understanding that they have acquired, simply in order to help us, is a lesson in itself of an unselfish wish to serve. For this mercy we should surely be much more grateful than we are, and make more effort to emulate their example and benefit by this privilege that they offer.

LIFE IS LIKE A VIOLIN

Much study and patient practise must be used to produce beautiful music from this instrument that will please the ear and lift the heart. Likewise in earthly life, much patient practise, study and effort must be given if you are to produce the music of life and love.

The knowledge and the understanding that you gain in your study of spiritual progression, is likened to the bow with which you play the violin. Play it gently, wisely and sensitively, and with knowledge, upon the strings of life, and you will experience the joy and achievement of beautiful living, the happiness that lifts the heart when truly beautiful music is played well.

You must not be disappointed if a string should break and cause difficulties for you. Every musician knows that difficulties will arise from time to time, but he who is well trained in skill and knowledge, also knows that the understanding of that knowledge will help to overcome all problems, and that faith in the hand that guides him will sustain and strengthen in any situation, no matter how difficult.

Difficulties that have been met and overcome strengthen and give valuable experience for the future, so that the player may be the better equipped to help not only himself as life unfolds, but also the better to understand the problems of others. The greater the experiences, the more beautiful the music will be, until the player is recognised as a master of his art.

THE COMMON DENOMINATOR

Think to consider how the evolution and progression of all things within the universe have many things in common, how everything follows – in its own way – a basic pattern of advancement.

The stars and suns of the universe, the rocks and formation of the crush of the earth, the personality of a human being from childhood to elderly states, the soul of every incarnate being – of every tree, flower, inhabitant of the animal kingdom, every tiny thought or wonderful idea. Each builds up from one tiny atom. Some take but a moment of time, some take billions of earthly years, but the process is the same. Strata upon strata, layer upon layer, builds up towards the perfect whole.

Here and there flaws appear, ruffling the continuity of creation. The mistakes cannot be eradicated, but must blend into the whole, so that even the mistakes of life and living become part of the complete picture. But by careful artistry, even the mistakes and errors of judgement can be used to enhance, giving the authenticity of genuine progression.

Mankind's own endeavours may seem infinitely small compared to the mighty structures of mountains, rivers and the vast plains of continents, but his task is still to build and evolve gradually, step upon step towards perfection in all he undertakes, whether it be a garden, a building, a mechanical appliance, his own earthly life or his own spiritual soul. Where mistakes are made and acknowledged, it is then for him to learn by it and blend it into his future, that it may become part of his achievement in such a way that it will enhance rather than detract. From every crack in the rocks, a flower can grow – given the time and artistry of nature, and man can do exactly the same with his own life and soul. Such is the plan of God.

★ ★ ★ ★ ★

We had been in our new home in North Devon for little more than two weeks, and as I looked out over the green patchwork of fields, where sheep were safely grazing, and to the wooded hill beyond, I was filled with the contented peace of this countryside. As I looked to my right, my gaze followed the winding course of the River Torridge, with its small boats rocking at safe anchorage, while the trees, fields and the homes of many other people, seemed to sweep graciously down to the river bank. All was silence, for it was early morning and I felt enveloped with the peace and tranquillity of the place. I turned to my left towards the rolling hillside, and there in the east I saw the streak of light that heralds the sunrise. The following lines came rushing to my mind and I had to return quickly to the bungalow to write them down lest I lose them altogether. The first verse I could remember, and as I wrote, the next verse followed, and the next, until the following poem was completed, all in a rather spidery handwriting that couldn't really be mistaken for my own. Somewhere beside me, above me, or inside my mind – I really know not where, another appreciative soul collected my own emotive feelings, and expressed them in words that I could never have found for myself, and added their own small portion of spirit wisdom.

THE LIGHT OF SPIRIT.

The streak of dawn peeps o'er the hill,
    To tell the night her task is done,
That God's own plan is working still,
    And darkness will be overcome.

This demonstration every morning,
    Renews our hopes for each new day,
For even as the sun is rising,
    This knowledge guides us on our way.

If we would know the power of Spirit,
   And use it for the good of man,
We would see with each new dawning,
   The loving power of Spirit's plan.

Rejoice all ye who glimpse the beauty,
   All who see the power of God,
All who know the path of duty,
   For you are blest with staff and rod.

And when another day is ending,
   And dusk is heralding the night,
Look towards the next dawn coming,
   Stand straight and tall towards the light.

★ ★ ★ ★ ★

REFLECTIONS UPON GENEROSITY

Hidden within the depths of every personality upon the earthplane, there is the true self, which often remains out of sight of every prying eye. This is a form of self protection which every soul uses to some extent, to keep itself free of undue influence from others who walk with them at various times along the pathway of earthly experience.

Each has his or her own route of life and understanding, each must gain their knowledge in their own way, and although there will be companions along that route, God in his wisdom enables us to keep our true selves to our own knowledge of ourselves, revealing to others such small particles as we wish from time to time. To those with whom we have the greatest rapport, we reveal more of our secret selves and give of ourselves more generously.

Part of the art of successful living upon the earthplane, is to know with whom you can share these fragments of inner self, and how best to share them with advantage to both, for each can learn from the other. It is part of the generosity of life that experience and knowledge thus gained, must be shared. It is part of the understanding of life to know that which you can take into your own inner self, and that which you should discard.

Some things should be discarded quickly, being of no use at all, apart from experiencing the awareness of their existence, whilst other knowledge and understanding is a priceless gift to be held and treasured for its use to yourself and others later on. The understanding required to sort the wheat from the chaff of experience, is the light of spiritual knowledge and truth which guides and protects that inner self, which is the secret soul that belongs to you alone. Only spirit shares your knowledge of this inner self, only God sees your conscience as an open book. Yet every incarnating soul and every discarnate being, draws from the same great source of loving power, so that each one, though privately individual is also part of the whole.

We now begin to realise the importance of sharing our lives and our knowledge. Some give of themselves wholeheartedly, their generosity of life shining brightly in a dark world of selfishness, where too many share no part of their inner selves with others, or even their more material acquisitions. The majority fluctuate between the two extremes.

The truly generous person is often unaware of this delightful trait of his or her nature, whilst those who give only in the material sense for personal gain, scarcely know the meaning of true generosity and very consciously pride themselves on their giving. Some exhibit a different angle of this spiritual gift when they acknowledge the achievements of another person who has a greater accomplishment in the same field of endeavour as their own, for jealousy could enter into these circumstances and dim the light of generosity.

It is those that give of themselves with a simple instinctive gesture of spontaneous love, without thought of gain or even acknowledgement, that express true spiritual generosity. Such souls may be found in all walks of life and position, wealth or poverty having no bearing on the quality of generosity. The man who gives much, but owns even greater, may well be less generous than he who gives little but offers all he has.

Of all the expressions of true generosity, time is one of the most valuable. Time is the only commodity of which everyone has an equal share to use as they can or wish during the twenty-four hours of each day. Some use it to good purpose, others do not. Often the busiest people will be the most generous with their time to help others, thus pinpointing the special generosity of their nature. It seems that he who has the least to spare, whether it be of time or wealth of some kind, is likely to be the most generous, almost as generous in fact, as the person who can forgive someone who has dealt them a severe disservice – a supreme manifestation of love, clothed in the beautiful gown of generosity. Whenever this special generosity of love reveals itself, it lights the way of life with a brightness that begins to emulate the cause of heaven.

It was an early morning in February, 1989. I was seated in my own special chair in our Rainbow Room, sorting through a folder of inspirational writings of previous years that we had found at the bottom of a drawer. I came upon an apparently blank sheet of paper, and suddenly experienced that now familiar urge to write – nothing in particular, just *write* I *must*.

Picking up my pen, I scribbled quickly an untitled piece about generosity and on completing the page and subject, put it aside. I never read immediately what I have written, as I find myself unable to concentrate on it properly. Later, on picking it up again, I noticed writing on the other side. This turned out to be some writing dated February 1985 entitled "Reflections On Generosity"! To my amazement, the writing of February 1989 followed the older piece without alteration, and the foregoing piece is the result.

I pondered on this little phenomenon for several days without coming to any spectacular conclusions. I only knew that it was yet another proof of the power, intent and organising ability of our spirit friends. I could only offer humble thanks for their tenacity and skill in bringing the subject matter to fruition as one complete piece of philosophy for the purpose of this book.

This incident was obviously not a case of my own memory ringing a bell, but the memory of a spirit friend with an inclination for writing, using their own memory to facilitate completion of the subject. Friends and relations often demonstrate the efficiency of their memory in the Spirit world, and use this means of proving their survival by jogging our own less reliable memories about some earthplane incident of the past – yet another example of the generosity of sharing, in this case a sharing between two worlds.

★ ★ ★ ★ ★

ONE LEG IN THE SKY

If you find yourself with a steadying hand upon the furniture as you stoop to retrieve something from the floor, then you are probably about my age. If you also find yourself on one leg with the other rising slowly as you bend forward, you are probably about the same weight as I am. If you are really determined to retrieve the fallen object, you may finish up with one leg rising towards the sky – always assuming you haven't toppled over in the process!

From this ballet-like position, it is interesting to note that although the eye sees all surrounding objects upside-down, the brain will conveniently turn them the right way up, and you know that all is well – the floor is still on the floor, the ceiling has not done an about-turn, but is still safely and securely overhead (if you were standing up of course), and that wonderful blue shelter – the sky, will also have remained unmoved by your own physical contortions.

Curiously, this half upended position can promote a good deal of profound thought – not least the fact that this situation is a strange reflection of life itself.

For instance, no matter what we think we see or hear, truth and indisputably proven facts remain the same. No matter from which angle you view an object or situation, it is in fact unchanged. It is only your views, opinions or conclusions which can alter. Isn't it a good thing that we keep one foot firmly on the ground, lest we land in an untidy heap on the lowest level of thought – the floor.

It seems to me that there are a number of interesting advantages in putting oneself periodically in this position of one leg in the sky. Physically it is a good exercise, metaphorically it has unlimited possibilities, not least amongst them the certainty of retaining one's sense of humour – an absolute necessity in this earthly life of ours, if we are not to succumb in a miserable, self-pitying pile of humanity at every adverse toss of the coin. If you can't laugh at yourself in this ridiculous position, you might as well give up.

Even more important of course is the knowledge that this unique position – again metaphorically speaking – helps us to see the other person's point of view, stops us jumping to inaccurate conclusions, opening the mind to wider possibilities, and above all, teaching us to retain a balance in all things. The whole thing has the added merit of costing us nothing!

Looking back upon my own life, it is easy to see now, how the often unwitting move of putting one leg in the sky has proved to be a great advantage. I have taken paths I am sure would have otherwise remained unexplored. I have seen what I was not intended to see in other people and often in situations. It has given me an understanding of man and beast in many diverse situations, and enabled me to derive from life a patient tolerance that I know would otherwise have escaped me.

Children of course frequently adopt this position of one leg in the sky as a matter of experiment, and usually as a preliminary to the more athletic stance of standing on one's head. From an early age, their physique and basic natural knowledge guides them towards these methods of development, physically, mentally and spiritually. They seem to have an in-built knowledge of some of the Yoga principles and positions. On reflection now, I think it a great pity that these instincts seem to fall by the wayside with increasing years. Perhaps as parents, we fall short in these matters. Most of us would I think stop our small children from standing on their heads in shops for instance, or other public places, and so the child begins to think of such practices as an error of judgment. If we took the trouble to explain why it is impractical to stand with one leg pointing skyward in public places and yet encourage it at home, our youngsters would learn much about general protocol at an early age and benefit greatly from the pursuance of such exercises for a much longer time, perhaps their entire lives.

For my own part, I was never an athletic child, and if I have a childhood regret, it is that I was never encouraged towards gymnastic and sporting attainments.

As I recall my schooldays in this respect, I remember doing quite well at netball and badminton, mainly because my head and shoulders were well above most of the other girls. In the case of netball, I didn't have to run about very much, merely hanging about in the region of the goal post, waiting for others to pass the ball for me to toss up into the net – I was nearly there anyway and stood a far better chance than my much shorter colleagues. It is a special kind of inbuilt wisdom that acknowledges one's limitations and makes sound use of any advantages we may have.

With badminton also, I was in an elevated position for sloshing that elusive little feathered shuttlecock straight over the net. In fact I was almost unbeatable at it. My only Waterloo occurred during our own private school championships, and was caused by the breaking of my knicker elastic rather than any extra skill on the part of my opponent. I recall quite clearly the feeling of panic that engulfed me on realising what had happened. The only plan I could think of was to lose the match as quickly as possible and escape to the cloakroom with a safety pin. As it turned out, it would have been quicker to win! I do feel now, that exercises such as one leg in the sky would have given me the confidence to take more positive action, instead of the negative solution I actually chose. After all, your gym knickers can't fall down if you are standing on your head! Ah well, so much for my 5 ft. 6½ ins. that were an important aspect of my life from the age of 10 onwards. I think I have now lost the extra half inch with advancing years, but in the schooldays of my life, my height was of considerable significance to me, sometimes to my advantage as I have explained, or more often to my disadvantage. How values change with passing years.

I remember it was a considerable contortion and source of misery to bob under the arms of other children whilst playing oranges and lemons at parties, which I disliked anyway. The memory is amusing now.

It is interesting to reflect upon the variety of upbringing of children and its effect upon them in later life. Undoubtedly the conditions of one's childhood have a profound effect on later life, although there does not seem to be any rule or guideline about this effect. A good, sound and happy upbringing does not always produce a good, sound and happy adult. Sometimes a child brought up in poverty of both material and emotional matters develops into a spiritually superior being, or overcomes the mundane disadvantages, to later become the embodiment of material success. The more you think about it, the more you realise that success or failure in any field of life is up to the individual. The way each person, young or old, reacts to their own particular circumstances, is the only criterion that decides the result. Each has the free will to choose their own reaction at whatever stage of their earthly lives. Each has personal responsibility to themselves to choose positive actions and go forward, or the negative ones that will hold them back in life. Perhaps too much emphasis is made these days on the influence of conditions and surroundings. Some will always rise above adversity in some way or other, others will never make good use of even the most favourable opportunities, whether they be opportunities of body, mind or soul.

For my own part, I had a happy childhood, shielded from much of the nastier side of life, and blessed with wonderful parents who always did the best they could for me according to their own knowledge and understanding. My father was cautious in the extreme, with sound moral principles that he seemed to base upon some wise thinking of his own, rather than any particular religious training. My mother was full of fun, left all business matters to my father, and added greatly to the pleasure and happiness of those around her. She was calmly willing to take on any situation that arose, and tackled each one with enthusiasm and understanding. Nothing seemed to ruffle my mother, and my father invariably 'came along too' in such matters, exhibiting an even greater calm within his own sphere of thought and action.

During our years with the Renegades Theatre Company, my parents' home had an open door for all and sundry concerning it. Jimmie (James Cooper), could arrive with whoever he felt inclined to bring – usually to help them in some way or other. Tea of the 'high' variety appeared from apparently nowhere, aided and abetted by Yvonne (Haesendonck) always willing to lend a hand and keep the work to a minimum for my mother.

After tea the table would be cleared, the washing up done amid much chatter and laughter. Then the fun would begin, with theatrical costumes in the making, the hand sewing machine burring at full speed, crêpe paper, flower wire and glue well in evidence, papier-maché would quite likely be around, being formed into sundry pantomime props – perhaps a lobster or cooked goose or ham. Pots and tins of poster paint lined up on the sideboard, Jane on the floor with rule and compass designing her latest stage creation. My father might be sawing a piece of wood, trying not to mark the table, though he occasionally did! Meanwhile Jimmie himself sat in the armchair nursing his script and pen, with one eye on the football match on the television screen. My mother would also take time off for this event, and she and Jimmie between them creating a fair atmosphere of excitement with yells of "GOAL" every now and then.

These were glorious days, when we all learnt much from one another, especially patience and tolerance I think. I often thought that my mother looked upon Jimmie as if he were the son she never had. And I know that he in turn gave her the love, thought and wisdom of his own experience, that he would have given to his own mother. I will explore my memory later concerning my theatre days, for at the moment I am still reflecting on some of my childhood memories and reactions.

Looking back now upon my early years, I realise that it was rather unfortunate that neither of my parents had any real knowledge of psychic matters. Of my father I wouldn't expect it, but my mother certainly was gifted to some extent in this respect. She always 'knew' when someone was coming to tea and who it was, although no prior arrangement had been made. She knew to the extent that she would prepare food and lay the table to accommodate the extra guests. But she was unaware that this was in any way unusual, and was equally unaware of my own psychic potential. She therefore did not believe in the real existence of my friends in our back garden. I had wonderful games with these spirit children and chatted away to them for hours on end, much preferring them to the worldly children at the front of the house, who seemed nice enough in their way, but a bit rough in their play by comparison. My mother used to 'tut' and mildly admonish me not to tell such fibs – according to her you see I never told lies, only fibs, which on reflection now suggests that she probably had an idea that there was some truth in my assertions, though she didn't understand what it was. I recall her telling kindly aunts and uncles that I had such a vivid imagination, by way of explanation of some of my more outrageous remarks no doubt.

But the lack of encouragement in my early life only delayed the psychic and spiritual development that came later, which demonstrates the patience of our Spirit Guides, who wait with understanding until we are ready to be used, and *that* time can only come when we wish it to be so. But there is ample proof that they can guide us towards it, and give us opportunities along the way. It is for us to accept them. Sometimes we fail to understand what is happening, and only in retrospect do we realise the opportunities we have used or missed.

My own opportunities came with an instinctive desire to heal, which I began to do without any actual knowledge of what was happening. The explanation and encouragement came via a work colleague who was both a medium and healer. Looking back, I can now clearly see each step of the way, planned and presented by Spirit. Every person needed to play a part, was in the right place at the right time. Incredible dovetailing of events culminated in my move to Christchurch in Dorset, where I met Ken whom I was to marry, and who was to provide the power needed for our spiritual work. Together we were able to produce our first book "Kaleidoscope of Living Thoughts" and a second book "I'm Jane", and now, still working together, we can offer the latest collection of Spirit thought and guidance. Neither of us had any previous idea of writing a book, in fact we were halfway through the first one before we received an indication that the material we had painstakingly recorded was intended to be printed – yet another example of the way in which Spirit can guide and inspire us, if only we will follow our instinctive thoughts, however extraordinary they may seem. So few things turn out to be exactly what they seem, which is perhaps another good reason for looking at situations from a variety of angles, even if it does mean a wobbly angle with one leg in the sky.

THE RHYTHM OF LIFE

All life has its own rhythm, and while that rhythm is maintained – all is well. If the rhythm is disrupted then things begin to go wrong. The rhythms of life may be counted in fractions of a second or in thousands of years. Most lie somewhere in between.

The moon and sun, stars and comets all appear with a regularity that differs with each one but is in accord with itself. Tides rise and fall according to its own rhythmic plan. While your heart beats with its own correct regularity you will not suffer a heart attack, but if it stumbles in its rhythm then something is wrong. If your clock upon the mantelpiece is ticking evenly to its own speed, it will tell you the truth about time, but if its ticks are uneven you cannot trust it.

All nature is particularly geared to a variety of rhythms. Seasons come and go each year, each with its own task towards life. There is a time to sleep, a time to awaken, a time to blossom and a time to slow down again for the preserving rest. Animals too have their rhythm by which they survive as individuals or the species. Only when their rhythms are interrupted or changed, often by the activities of mankind, do things begin to go wrong.

Through the years man has increasingly interrupted the rhythms of nature, farming in particular has manipulated the rhythms of livestock and growing crops, thus opening the door for many problems.

If just one instrumentalist in an orchestra does not play at the correct tempo, all the other players are disrupted and discord replaces harmony, which demonstrates the far reaching results of one person getting out of rhythm with his or her fellow players in the orchestra of life.

It is quite possible to improve the health of body, mind and soul by rhythmic exercise or dancing. The extent of the action is of little consequence, it is the rhythm and flow of the movement that will create an inner harmony. One has only to watch an experienced ballet dancer to appreciate the value of rhythmic flowing movement. If people would live their lives according to the pattern and rhythm that is right for them, much sorrow and disappointment could be avoided.

Native populations in unexplored jungles have always known the value of rhythm, and their dancing action has been in accordance with whatever result they were seeking. So called civilized man seems to be losing the knowledge of the value of rhythm and is therefore in danger of losing his civilization with it. If mankind would but recreate the art of using rhythm in his thoughts and actions, then daily life and living would flow peacefully with God.

Sometimes the rhythm of ones life is dislocated by the thoughts or actions of another person, but even in these circumstances the effects are minimised if there was a good positive rhythm of life in the first place, for it is then far easier to restore that equilibrium. Most people underestimate the value of rhythm, but when deeper thought is given to its many aspects, it is quickly realised that it is an important part of natural law, and the basis of God's creation. It then becomes obvious that it is more rewarding to live and think within the guidelines of nature, it is a happier and healthier existence that is lived with, rather than against the rhythm of life.

FEBRUARY GARDEN

Icicles hang glowing pink
   Reflected from the morning sun,
February's icy link,
   Hiding all the joys to come
– After winter's frost.

A snowdrop hangs her modest head,
   Her green tips blending with the grass.
When other flowers feign they're dead,
   The brave young snowdrop shows her class
– And challenges the frost.

Last year's brown and shrivelled leaves
   Offer shelter to the birds,
While others warm beneath our eaves,
   Accept our crumbs and kindly words,
– Till the passing of the frost.

But 'neath the quilt of shining white,
   Beneath the frozen crust of earth,
Nature plans a summer bright
   With flowers rejoicing in rebirth,
– With no memory of frost.

The February branches bare,
   Make lacy patterns 'gainst the sky.
A bird of passage, seen but rare,
   Shows us mortals how to fly
– To beat the winter frost.

Yet catkins wag their tails with glee,
   And silver pussy willow tips
Promise winter's cold will flee,
   Recycle time to haws and hips,
– Before next winter's frost.

All our earthly lives are run,
   By nature's ever circling time,
Our days are blest with warming sun
   When we have overcome the rime
– And thoughts of winter frost.

★ ★ ★ ★ ★

TO START THE DAY
(A morning Prayer)

Dear Father in Thy Holy name,
Please hear this prayer from me,
That I may live this day the same
As you would have me be.

Please help me live my life today,
Thy love within me stirred,
That I may walk the Spirit way
According to Thy word.

Please help me smile if things go wrong,
And to offer helping hands.
To sing a joyful, happy song –
Walk tall to life's demands.

Please help me guide another soul,
To give it peace and rest,
Fulfil my own true earthly role,
And humbly do my best.

Bless all those who seek to be
Instruments of Thy peace,
And help all earthly eyes to see
That turmoil now can cease.

Lord, lend Thy wisdom to this earth,
That we may reap Thy knowledge,
To give each day love's own rebirth,
Which we may live with courage.

Amen.

★ ★ ★ ★ ★

LIFE IS BUT A GARDEN

On 19th February, 1987, at 7.48 in the morning, the following communication for inclusion in this book, was received in trance from our Communicator who we call "Friend".

"Friend" gave us the major part of our first book *Kaleidoscope of Living Thoughts,* which is entirely concerned with the philosophy of life and spirit teachings. He has been with us ever since to offer his words of wisdom when needed.

This wonderful guide, so knowledgeable himself, is the link between ourselves and other even higher minds. We believe our Communicator was not of English origin and may have been on the earth so many years ago that our modern English would not come easily, so that the phrasing may sound a little strange to our readers, certainly different in places, but it is interesting to observe that this improved very much with time and usage.

His explanations often revolve around flowers and other aspects of nature, in an attempt to translate the knowledge of highly evolved souls into language and circumstances that we can readily understand, which is demonstrated here:–

All life is but a garden, both on your plane of life and here in the world of Spirit. As you know, a garden can be a very beautiful place. It may be a formal garden, designed by experts, where everything is under complete control, and many beautiful flowers, trees and shrubs will live and flourish there, perhaps beyond their natural beauty, or out of their normal environment, with the aid of the gardeners. There are also wild gardens, where beautiful simple wild flowers flourish, and the trees and bushes give their beauty and their shelter to all nature that lives within them. But even these must be tended. Unless the gardener keeps his wild garden under proper control, it becomes a wilderness, here the strong stifles the weaker, and justice no longer occurs, and many lovely smaller flowers and plants will be stifled and overcome by the stronger and rougher growth.

In life too, you see this same pattern. Some lives are orderly, are pruned to special designs. Other lives are much less formal, more unrestrained with a different kind of beauty or pattern. In both cases it is for the individual gardeners to control their lives – their gardens – to the utmost advantage for their spiritual progression.

The type of garden that your life becomes is entirely up to the individual, to you as the gardener in charge of that life. If you find you are not succeeding, maybe you should give thought that you are trying to develop the wrong kind of garden. Perhaps you are trying to build the formal beauties of the great and wonderful gardens of your world. It could be that it is ego which tries to overcome the natural instincts and makes a person try to be what they are not. Perhaps their garden would be more productive, more beautiful if it were represented by the dainty bluebells and simple primroses, all the wild flowers and shy ferns that grow so profusely, and give such light and pleasure in uncultivated places, if they are allowed to do so. If those who feel they are failing in life, would give this comparison some thought, they may find they could be more successful with a different kind of garden of life.

Even the jungles of the world are controlled to a large measure by the life that is within them. The animals that use them become gardeners of their own domain in an instinctive way, sometimes they better succeed than the human being who struggles with the wrong kind of garden, for the animal is in its natural environment.

Here in our Spirit World, similar patterns evolve, and people can live here according to their knowledge and progression, in the kind of garden that they have created for themselves whilst on the earthplane. Those with darker, muddled thinking, or perhaps evil thoughts, have built a garden of wilderness, uncontrolled, where tendrils trip them as they try to break through the confusion of their own making, where the overhanging growth makes darkness and despair.

Such people, such souls, can come away from the wilderness whenever they choose, into the light, and build a happier garden of flowers, as there is always a guiding helper to assist them as soon as they become conscious of the true wish, but the choice is their's here, even as it is upon your plane of life.

Gardeners are near to nature, they have an inner understanding of life that some others lack. Those who work the soil, and see the beauty in the simple things that it brings forth, as well as the majesty of fine old trees and the grand landscape of the whole, have made a great step forward, for in seeing and understanding these things, they can see a small glimpse of the light and love of the Great Creator, the purity and love of Spirit. They may not recognise it as such in many cases, but the fertile seed of knowledge is there, and they will readily understand when the opportunity is acknowledged.

And so dear friends, when you toil in a garden, sometimes in sunshine, but often in cold winds and frost, or deplore the heavy rains that make your soil seem unworkable, remember, these are but the toils of life, and from these toils will come great beauty and many fruits – if you use the opportunities and your knowledge aright. Bless you my friends, bless you.

THE LONELY HEART

Loneliness is the greatest single cause of unhappiness and despair. It has been so throughout the ages of mankind, who seems to be unable to solve this problem to any substantial degree. The reason is not hard to find, for loneliness has a different cause and effect for every individual person, and no matter what others do to help, in the end the cure is within the one that is lonely, others are only in a position to help them overcome the difficulty.

To a very lonely person, this brief summary may seem harsh and unfeeling, but it is not so, it is a basic truth that has to be faced before loneliness can be finally banished – and it can. This is surely a worthwhile task, so let us look more closely at loneliness in the fervent hope that amongst our readers there will be some who will be helped by the words we offer from Spirit.

The situations that foster loneliness are many and varied. We will consider some of these, in the hope that some who read our words will recognise the circumstances – the first steps towards overcoming the lonely situations that they are currently enduring.

The most obvious cause of a lonely state of mind is the physical loss of someone near and dear. This may be because of bereavement or a permanent parting through earthly cause, divorce for example, or a parting between mother and child when adoption is arranged. There are many explanations for permanent physical partings, and one fact remains common to all of them. If there was true love on the part of one for the other, then a great sense of loss will be experienced which sometimes seems unbearable – loneliness.

Then there is the loneliness that can be acutely known in a crowd. This will seem a strange thought to many. The outgoing nature of many people enables them to feel comfortable in a crowd, giving a sense of security that they would miss on their own. But many other people walk into a crowded room and feel more lonely than they would if it were empty. Even if they actually know some of those present, their own retiring nature will not allow them to go forward, to interrupt someone else's conversation, or even let their presence be registered in any way at all. This loneliness has a basic cause of fear, of a feeling of inadequacy, not necessarily because that person is in fact inadequate, but sometimes simply because their own knowledge is different from that of the other people present − as far as they know. The fear may emerge as evidence that they really have not the courage to explore other people's knowledge, or perhaps be on an entirely different level of thinking.

A very sensitive person will often avoid crowded places, simply because they are very apt to pick up subconsciously the thoughts and vibrations of other people, and in a crowded place it is almost inevitable that some of those people will be out of tune with them, and this can be a very uncomfortable experience, so here again, the sensitive person can experience a feeling of isolation in a crowded room, and a deep seated fear of this can make matters worse than they need be, and a dreadful loneliness will envelop that person.

Disability is another heartbreaking cause of loneliness, because in addition to the loneliness, that person is also trying to deal with physical difficulties of a kind they may never have known before. Someone who has previously led an active life and been largely independent of another helping hand, may become ill or injured in such a way that they suddenly find themselves dependant on others for so much they took for granted as their own prerogative before. The everyday tasks of life, both large and small, suddenly become major situations, and there may not always be someone at hand to help. However many friends or relations that person has, however willing and anxious to help they may be, there will be times when no-one is there. The person has to manage as best they can alone for at least some of the time, and experiences a devastating loneliness that no-one else can understand, unless they have themselves lived alone under such circumstances. The mere frustrations emphasise that loneliness a hundred times a day. Even if there is someone living with them and caring for them, the personal dependence upon another isolates them mentally and still creates that lonely feeling of despair.

The majority of people can freely walk into churches, clubs and places of entertainment. But if they do not know anybody there, they can feel very lonely in such places. If you cannot even get to them by yourself, the isolated feeling is increased.

There is another side to this particular coin. There are situations in life where a disability for one person will prompt attention and kindly action from others, that would not have been offered in normal circumstances, simply because they could not see a need, and so the one with the disability is given a chance to accept both gratefully and graciously the kindly overtures. But where a disability is not readily obvious, then the sympathy and consequential action will not so easily be forthcoming – because the need is not seen, and here we can realise the possibility of acute loneliness.

These are but a few examples of loneliness and serve to demonstrate the variety and complexity of this unhappy state. When we realise that many people can happily spend a considerable amount of time alone in quiet isolated places, we begin to realise that loneliness is not so much the result of circumstances, but an unrest within the mind. Circumstances may well have triggered the condition into an active state, but it is the way we accept and deal with these circumstances that makes the difference between peace of mind, isolated moments of loneliness, or a life lived in dull despair.

If we lose a much loved physical presence and grieve for a while, it is nothing of which to be ashamed – it is a natural and probably a healing and essential part of life, but we have to realise that our loved one is well and happy in their new life and we on earth are really in sorrow for ourselves – perfectly normal for us all, but prolonged for too long, we bring sorrow to the loved one who has passed to Spirit, and create our own dark thoughts and gloom for ourselves. We can quite easily isolate ourselves from our loved ones who would want to help us, whether it be from the World of Spirit or from those upon the earthplane. If we reject the offered help, we frustrate their efforts on our behalf and make ourselves more lonely with every passing day. Those in Spirit may then find it impossible to help us no matter how much they wish to do so. Friends upon the earthplane will give up their attempts and turn to other avenues where their efforts bring forth better fruits.

Sometimes it is hard for someone still in earthly conditions to realise the grief of another. Many for instance would not understand the loneliness of a person who has lost a much loved pet. But this too creates in some an extreme sense of loss and loneliness. The nature of the loss has little to do with the situation – it is the degree of love and understanding that was shared in earthly life that determines the emotional upheaval involved. It would be a mistake to judge a person's feeling of loss. For some the greatest loss would be a marriage partner, for some a parent, child or friend, for others it may well be a dog or cat perhaps. Best not ask or question why, but simply offer all the help you can. If you are the one who grieves, raise your thoughts above your pain, ask for help and guidance, and be prepared to accept and work on the help that comes. The more you try, the more the help will present itself and the less difficult it will become to rise above the sorrow. The effort will automatically attract even more help – from both worlds – and you will find you have created around you a circle of light and friendship that dispels all thought of loneliness in due course.

Whatever the problems that appear to create loneliness, we always have to look within ourselves for the answer. The blame is never elsewhere, we have to recognise our own failings and seek to overcome them each in our own way, and one very good way is to try to help another. Perhaps someone with a similar problem to our own, or it could be something quite different. We all have experiences in our lives that teach us as we pass along, and it is for each to use the knowledge gained to help others, by doing so we help ourselves, until we too can stand in some quiet place, and hear the silence with contentment, and be at one with the circumstances we have. When we have trained ourselves to help and be helped, we can know the peace of mind that has no room for loneliness, for once you become aware of Spirit guidance and understanding, and accept the help so gladly offered, you nurse a secret knowledge that protects you and enables you to share the love that surrounds you with those people that you meet in daily life. In sharing that love and friendly feeling with others, you draw more love towards yourself, more friendliness, until you find quite suddenly that you are truly living once again – a different life perhaps for many – the next and new experience that is part of life on earth.

Courage is the strength and power to mend a breaking heart, knowledge is the spark that lights the way for courage to work the magic spell that takes away the ache of loneliness, and helps the heart to sing again, in tune and harmony with life.

ENCOURAGEMENT

Oh noble heart be strong,
And lift your eyes to God.
You stand where you belong,
Equipped with staff and rod.

Your higher thoughts ascend,
To greet that inner peace.
Unselfish love will mend,
And bring a sweet release.

The greater gift of life
And understanding love,
Can overcome all strife,
Bring guidance from above.

Be still and hear the song
Of Spirit's loving care,
To shield you from all wrong,
And all your life to share.

THE COMING OF SPRING

See here the swelling leafbuds greet the spring,
White hoarfrost melts, revealing everything
The shining mantle has been sheltering,
And once again the birds begin to sing.

The winter aconite feels braver now
That greenish tips appear on every bough,
And primrose shows the promise of her vow
To clothe the banks and woodlands with her flower.

And we can see the power of God's hand,
Life's mystery in every grain of sand
That moulds the soil into a fertile land,
And stirs the coming spring at His command.

★ ★ ★ ★ ★

LAUGHTER IS THE BEST MEDICINE

There is nothing new in the knowledge that laughing is good for you, for it not only spells happy thinking, it actually relaxes the mind and body. Tightened muscles of the face, neck, shoulders and hands automatically relax when you laugh. Certainly many a taut situation sags into proper proportions when a sense of humour comes to the rescue, and many a potentially explosive occasion has been defused in the same way.

Throughout this book readers will find touches of humour amongst the wisdom of Spirit, and some readers may even feel that this is inappropriate. I hope not, for kindly laughter teaches us much, helps us to be more tolerant and understanding and above all, can create a bond where no other exists, and open doors that would otherwise remain forever closed.

The important criteria for humour and healing laughter is that it must be for the right reason. Motive is just as important for laughter as everything else that we do in this earthly life. It matures with our increasing years, and it is vital that it develops in the right way for our own spiritual development, otherwise we harm ourselves and others with the prickly barbs of unkind humour and laughter.

This is easy to see in the undeveloped humour of most children. Their simplicity of mind sees the funny side of someone else's misfortune, which is the basic joke of slipping on a banana skin, the well aimed custard pie or bucket of water in the circus ring. Many an adult sense of humour stays at least partly at that level, though some of these develop a more sophisticated version of the same type of humour – the sardonic wit of words that is designed to bring about the downfall of another in a special and temporary way – the banana skin of words, or more subtly perhaps, the custard pie of phrases.

Clearly this is not a healing humour, rather a quick crack of a wordy whip, basically designed to hurt. It stems from the worldly mind, is processed by a worldly brain to use in earthly circumstances to the detriment of others. Whereas the kindly humour of an evolved spirit never hurts or seeks to use that humour to take a rise over others. Here we find humour and laughter used to heal and lighten a situation that might otherwise remain in darkness. Even so, circumstances can alter any given situation. No-one for example would think it funny if a crippled old lady with a walking stick slipped on the banana skin and fell. But if the old lady was in fact a man caricaturing a crippled old lady and dressed as one, and *he* slipped and fell because of the banana skin, a great many people would laugh uproariously, knowing full well that the disguised man was going to fall deliberately to amuse and be quite capable of doing so safely. A few souls of deeper thinking might find it unfunny to even imitate a crippled person in this way, which demonstrates the delicate differences in the art of having a sense of humour, and perhaps the differences in the sensitivity of the true self of each person and the spiritual development expressed through humour.

Very occasionally one comes across a completely undeveloped humour, where a deliberate trap is set up to cause embarrassment or shock for one person, to the amusement of others, often causing pain or injury to the victim – the suddenly pulled away chair, fireworks through letter boxes or pushing a non-swimmer into deep water are examples of this type of cruel and undeveloped humour. The deliberate firing of unkind words, disguised thinly in the gay wrappings of humour, come into this category too, the cruel barbs, like arrows of discontent, finding their mark to the amusement of some others of like mind. These avenues of laughter are not healers, they seek to hurt and destroy for some dark inner purpose of their own.

From these thoughts it is easy to see that laughter, like everything else, can be used for good or ill, and it is entirely up to the individual how this gift is used. A gift it certainly is, although few people will think of it in that way.

And so, this book is dotted here and there with this priceless, uplifting type of thinking, so that lighter, clearer understanding may evolve through its pages, that the joy of living may come where previously there was no joy, and all who read it may rediscover something that they knew instinctively as a child – laughter heals and can lift vibrations to a higher plane. It can give us – with our greater knowledge of the passing years – a true appreciation of a wisely and kindly developed sense of humour which must begin with an ability to laugh at ourselves. It is surprising how many otherwise experienced people have not learnt to do this, but when this art has been accomplished, the stage is set to help others with that magic touch of kindly humour – the curtain rises on a play of true and happy laughter that infects the entire audience, whether it be of one or hundreds. 'Laugh and the world laughs with you – weep and you weep alone'.

Spontaneous laughter from a situation will usually bring the best results, the scripted joke being either too predictable or open to sarcastic and unkindly wit, for there are so many kinds of humour, enough in fact to suit all tastes and stages of development. But in the end, they all are based on one of two approaches. The anticipated climax, which you know is coming and for which the brain awaits in anticipation, thus the banana skin and custard pie and their wordy counterparts. The other being the surprise humour, or unexpected word or situation, and this is the aspect of humour that will be so helpful when it comes from a well developed soul because it will be influenced by a force outside that person. Someone with a gift of poetry for example, can easily be influenced by a spirit entity who can help them to express beautiful or humorous thoughts in the flowing metres of poetry, the mere rhythm of the lines creating a harmonious atmosphere of mind. But let it not be forgotten that all those in the world of Spirit are not necessarily of kindly thinking. If on the earthplane those souls were of sharp and unkindly wit, they would seek someone still upon the earth through whom they can work and express themselves.

So once again we are back to our own personal responsibility. The necessity of training our own minds in kindness and tolerance towards others – to lift our own minds to a higher level of appreciation and understanding, and thereby opening ourselves to the thoughts, skills and influence of more evolved spirits, who wait so patiently to help us and use us for good purposes. Humour of the right kind is undoubtedly a valuable and healing gift that prescribes this very potent medicine – laughter.

The following poem came in a flush of words and lines, on a variety of scraps of paper, as I went about my daily tasks – several days before the foregoing article about laughter. I afterwards realised that the poem was in fact intended to appear after it – one of the tongue-in-cheek little jokes that my Spirit friends often share with me – putting things back to front! to my amusement and I think to theirs.

THE JOKE'S ON ME!

When I really try to be
Fit and slim as a sapling tree,
Something always will go wrong,
And bring about a sad wee song.

When the pounds all disappear,
And fluent movements comes to bear,
And I should be all fairy light
It seems that I don't feel so bright.

The sparkle seems to hide away,
And won't come back until the day
When bulges re-appear all round,
And happiness is pound for pound.

When walking up a hill I pant,
And move around like an elephant,
I feel as happy as a lark,
Although to fly is not my mark!

I've cycled miles on the bedroom floor,
Bent and danced till my joints are sore,
I've counted calories every day,
There's nothing left to do but pray!

Why *is* it that, I once was slim,
With every part of me so trim,
While pounds now cling and firmly hold –
At least I now don't feel the cold!

Sometimes I think I will give up
The fight to be like a one year pup.
Perhaps true fitness will not come
Till heaven is my happy home.

For no-one can be heavy there,
Nor be clumsy, or despair,
For they would fall right back to earth –
Sheer weight would give them second birth!

Perhaps I'll settle for half way,
And live to laugh another day,
Just semi-fat I think will do,
That others may laugh with me too.

Every life should have some fun,
Cheer and smiles for everyone.
If I succeed by being fat,
Then that's my line – and *that* is *that!*

THE SWINGS AND ROUNDABOUTS OF TIME

Mortal thinking is so impatient. Few upon the earthplane are fully conscious of the modesty of time – very few indeed. Mostly the individuals of earthly existence hurry and rush at almost everything they do. Even those who have adopted a gentler pace, find they have to gear their tasks to accommodate and fit into the clock arrangements of others.

This appears to be a necessity for a well organised life upon the earthplane. In its own way, it helps to create a harmony on earth, by exercising a discipline in thought and consideration for others, avoiding disrupting confusions, and in general keeping an organised balance in the order of earthplane life and thinking. All of this concerns material things and material life, but there is another aspect of time that requires a different understanding and thinking – time in relation to Spirit.

There are more aspects of time of course, but these are enveloped in the mysteries of science, yet to be slowly revealed to mankind as he searches and blunders, enquires and succeeds.

Although time in our world of Spirit is non-existent by earthly measurement, it is still of importance when communication towards the earthplane is required. It may be necessary to steer an incarnate soul to a certain place at a certain time in order to be available to receive that communication. It may be desired that a certain person shall be given an opportunity of some kind, for them to make spiritual progress. That opportunity must coincide with that person's presence in the right place – and again – at the right time. There are endless examples that could be given, these two will suffice to demonstrate the need for those of us who are in Spirit, to be conscious of earth-time, and in these two instances, very precise timing would be necessary.

People living their daily lives in earthplane conditions, can have no conception whatsoever of the difficulties that have to be overcome to create such precise timing on the earthplane, simply because the earthplane existence is so tightly geared to its own time.

Often, comparatively little thought is given by those on the earthplane to assist those in Spirit to overcome these enormous problems. Many people meet on a regular basis to assist spirit communication. Even those attending orthodox church services, unwittingly are making themselves available for Spirit to communicate with them on this regular basis, and a sensitive person may well be aware sometimes of Spirit's presence. The regularity of any such meeting, whether it be a thousand persons or just one, can only be of help to those in Spirit to carry out their own part in such a contact.

Of greater importance, is when a group of people sit specifically for the purpose of being available for Spirit communication. It is necessary for them to honour that arrangement, as indeed those in Spirit will honour it, for it should be understood that those of us in the Spirit World attempt these communications when we feel it is necessary or desirable, and this can only be assessed from this side of life. There is insufficient power upon earth to 'call up' Spirit communicators at earthplane will or fancy. Yet there are those who will alter the arrangement on quite flimsy excuse, little realising the wasted effort of Spirit, the unproductive power that has been used, not only from a Spirit source, but possibly power from others on the earthplane connected with the arrangement. Failure to honour such arrangements are not only a waste of time, but are a discourtesy that would not be readily accepted between earthplane persons only. But in our world of Spirit we do not condemn nor criticize, merely sorrow and patiently await further opportunities.

Most people carry a timepiece upon their persons. Most also have others around their homes and places of work and play. There are often clocks on buildings, in motor cars and railway stations, and many other places where time is of importance to those going about their daily business. All these reminders of time, emphasize the importance of it towards well organised living. Yet still the late comers slip through half open doors as quietly as they can, thereby indicating their guilty conscience in the matter of timekeeping, or totally disregarding the interruptions they are causing, and thereby revealing their own insensitivity and their lack of spiritual consciousness. A person's attitude to time reveals a great deal about that inner consciousness.

When people are gathered together for the purpose of being available to Spirit, such transgressions can be very upsetting, for if all else fails to disrupt a meditative quietness, a squeaky door will certainly do so, showing that someone has failed to attend to this modest but important task of punctuality, that helps smooth communication and assistance from the Spirit World – a minor discourtesy perhaps, but nevertheless an indication of the lack of understanding by some upon the earthplane towards the Spirit World. Yet Spirit never fails, never retaliates, never despairs.

We seek to help those who struggle upon the earthplane towards better and more conscientious thought and action. We do not blame, we support. We do not judge, but weep when earthly souls discard us, and we wait with a patience beyond your comprehension for the erring soul to awaken to the brighter light of spiritual progress, for time is, as you see, of no importance in the world of Spirit.

On the earthplane, life is so controlled by time, that more people should be conscious of its true uses – to facilitate orderly living – to encourage the kinder aspects of human nature, the courtesy of thought and action towards others, the gift of ones own valuable time to those in need. Time can be a hindrance if you let it be so, or can smooth the path of life, can heal old wounds and sorrows. It brings about your yearly seasons, with alternating glory in garden, woodland, hill and vale.

Many people seem determined to fill every moment of every day, rushing from one thing to another, without giving themselves a brief pause for reflection. In the process, they wear out mind and body, often with results that do not justify the sacrifice. Wiser, more thoughtful use of time would bring greater accomplishments.

What great advantage it would be to mankind, if pause were made to reflect upon time, and thus lift themselves above the mundane things of life upon the earthplane. What great advantages there would be if the wondrous gift of time was fully appreciated and wisely used, for boredom would be unknown, the darker side of life and thought would diminish from recognition, and time would prove to be the great healer that in reality – it is.

WORKING WITH NATURE

The serenity and beauty of nature are only limited by the activities of mankind. The glory and peace of nature are fenced off only by the mind of man. Mankind can open the gate to gracious living and thinking any time he chooses, by opening his mind to the sanctified beauty and peace of nature – which is Spirit – which is God.

Destroy the individuality of each component part, and you destroy the material with which you could make the whole, for you have upset the balance provided for you to use. Nature demonstrates the use of perfect balance and mankind should use her example instead of continually seeking to destroy it, thereby putting great pressure upon natural reserves in order to restore that essential balance. Working *with* nature could bring about much happiness and progression for the souls of the earth plane, and thereby, those in the world of Spirit.

By thinking in a spiritual way towards the conservation of his world, mankind can work with nature and keep that essential balance intended by his own creator. Destroy that balance beyond the point of no return, and the very essence of the planet is set upon a path of deterioration and destruction.

It is the choice of mankind to decide the destiny of the earth. All life upon it will survive as Spirit, but the inanimate ingredients of basic material can only survive in the different form that must occur if its present construction is crumbled.

God has the power, but mankind has the choice, whether or not to use that power and love of God to good purpose by working with nature. Mankind's own free will can manifest itself by choosing the progressive path of nature's proper balance – the difference between night and day, the battle between good and evil, the acknowledgement of God's power in the recognition of His natural resources and the loving preservation of them.

Wise indeed is the soul that recognises the power and love of God through nature, wiser still is the mind that seeks to use that knowledge to maintain the balance that can preserve its very existence on earth.

BIRTH OF LIFE

The roots of life are deep within
   The very soul of man,
The leaves of life spring forth from roots,
   Propelling the greater plan.
And after leaves, the flowers spring
   The opportunities of life,
Some will form a sweet bouquet,
   Some will fade with strife.

But those that live will bear the fruits
   If nurtured with loving care,
To feed the very soul of man
   That brought the fruit to bear.
The circle of all life responds
   To thinking that is right,
Born of truth and sincerity
   Upon the wings of light.

A MARCH GARDEN

Could they but dare, the buds of March,
To stir beneath the dark tree bark,
And peep into the dawn of day,
For spring is not so far away,
And trees will clothe again in green
From those brown buds that were unseen.

Some daffodils begin to nod
Golden heads from soil untrod.
Biting March winds slope their stalks,
To sway and dance in ballet walks.
They catch the sunshine through the trees,
Give hope of summer, just to tease.

For summer sun is future still,
But tiny brown seeds, can and will
Produce our flowers and fruits of soil,
If Marchtime is our planting toil.
For we must play our own true part,
To stir again the sleeping heart.

★ ★ ★ ★ ★

GRATITUDE – A DIFFERENT OPPORTUNITY

Gratitude is easy in the light of beauty and the good things of life. It is harder to have gratitude for the darker and difficult moments of our span. But if those who suffer in any way at all – perhaps at the institution of acts from others – if such events can be accepted as a challenge, as opportunities for progression of the soul, that the spirit may rise above them and therefore towards God, then my friends you have the opportunity to be grateful for these things too. You have the opportunity to be grateful for difficulties in life, as well as the wonders and the joys.

Sometimes, some people prefer this shorter route towards a higher evolvement for their own soul. Some people like to climb high rocky mountains, others prefer the gentler, longer routes.

Suffering in one person gives an opportunity of service to another, by caring for that person and giving the help they may need. Any experience of either kind is a matter for which we can be truly grateful – yet another opportunity that does not always spring readily to mind.

No easy task to be grateful for upsets or even disasters, but in the realisation that adversity gives us such wonderful opportunities for greater and quicker progression of the soul, it is a great comfort and upliftment to know that our guides and helpers are ever with us to help in such a mammoth task.

Should we choose a different path and lay gratitude aside, they will not blame us or withhold support. We merely postpone the lesson, or receive it in some other way that we may find, as individuals, more acceptable, and more within the limits of our own strength. It is for us to choose.

TO OUR OWN SELVES BE TRUE

Shakespeare's plays are so full of quotable quotes – steeped in the wine of wisdom – that it can be an interesting and worthwhile exercise to let the mind wander amongst some of the words he gave to the characters in his plays.

We find for instance in his play Hamlet, Prince of Denmark, this advice: '. . . This above all, to thine own self be true; and it must follow, as the night the day, thou canst not then be false to any man.' What a wise philosophy of life.

If we paused to think about it, how often would we catch ourselves out with an uncharitable thought, word or action. So often it has happened before we have time to stop it, which we certainly would if we could, because we would know that we have not been true to ourselves or our spiritual beliefs.

How many terrible deeds have been perpetrated in the past and present, in the name of religion? Most religions have a spiritual basis of some kind, but because some of the followers of those religions are not true to their own beliefs, sincerity becomes non-existent and chaos reigns, with dreadful results in fear, suffering and intolerance.

We cannot of course expect to make the world right overnight, or even in our own lifetime, but we *can* set a good example. By being true to ourselves, our own beliefs and consciences, we can give others pause for thought, thus opening up a whole new way of thinking for others around us, giving hope where at present there seems none.

We must not be disappointed if our efforts often seem to fall on stony ground, for a few seeds of our knowledge will land on more fertile soil, and these will take root and grow in due course. We may not see the results ourselves, it may be someone else's task to see the harvest and help gather it together. But we can be happy in the certainty that we have done our best towards a better, peaceful world in the future, simply by being true to ourselves and our own beliefs now.

When enough people of this earthplane realise this truth and act upon their knowledge, enormous strides forward will be made. Meanwhile, our own personal steps can lead in the right direction so that others can follow, and be true to themselves – and thereby to others.

Some other words of wisdom from The Bard . . . "that which we call a rose, by any other name would smell as sweet." Perhaps we are at times too concerned about the opinions other people have of us – we worry how they will think and speak of us, perhaps giving a wrong impression – oh how we fear that we may be misunderstood.

And yet, when we come to the important truth of the matter, our only concern should be that we are kind, honest and upright in our way of life and thinking. For to God other peoples' opinions do not count, our own truth is between Him and our own consciences – no-one else. If our way of life is truly like the rose, then it will be as beautiful in the eyes of God, despite any other label that mere people pin upon us.

This brings us back to our title . . . "To our own selves be true" . . . for if we are, then any other name, opinion or accusation cannot change it. A rose we are and will remain, while we are true to God through truth within ourselves.

Our third search amongst Shakespeare's gems of thought, might well produce this observation – "All the world's a stage, and all the men and women merely players; they have their exits and their entrances and one man in his turn plays many parts".

Appropriately, it comes from "As You Like It" for truly do we choose the parts we play through life and truly they are many. Apart from the obvious differences in our way of life that change with increasing age, we find our way of thinking altering not only with time but also with circumstances.

We can even present more than one face to the world at any one given period of our lives. A man may for instance, act out the part of a senior managerial position whilst earning his daily bread, then at the end of the day return home to become a father sharing his children's playtime. He may then go out to enjoy his own leisure time at some sport that appeals to him. Three entirely different faces to present to the world at large, cast in three different roles that are played to different audiences at the same period of his life, and yet all three can be true reflections of the man.

Often people present a false face to the world, sometimes with wrong intent to deceive, perhaps for personal gain, at other times it is merely an innocent cover of true feelings or circumstances to spare another some distress. We hear of people who hide a serious illness or some other trouble from a loved one in order to spare them worry and unhappiness. Here the 'actor' must play the part with great conviction if the partner is to be deceived in this well meant way, for a sensitive soul can often collect the thoughts and feelings of people around them, especially if there is a close bondage between them, and this must surely be a forgivable deceit with such a motive.

As time goes on, with increasing opportunities to gain and use our spiritual knowledge, we realise our own responsibility to play each part to the best of our ability and with integrity, for life, just like the play has many actors in it, and some of those actors will be in partnership with us, depending on us to give a good performance, for acting, whether it be on theatre's stage or on the stage of life, is a matter of teamwork, a sharing for a while whatever circumstances we find around us.

We enter and exit all the phases of our lives as best we may, and do the best we can with the script we are given to enact between the two. Our best performances will be when we are sincere in what we do and say, with due consideration for our fellow actors. The script, designed by God, and the setting chosen by ourselves before we came to earth, is there for us to use, only the players can spoil the performance. But if we are to our own selves true, then we shall not be false to any man, neither will we be false to God.

THE TOLERATION FACTOR

Toleration – that double sided principle that can make or break any situation, be it for good or ill.

*In*tolerance is probably the most common basic cause of trouble in our world. From petty squabbles and misunderstandings in our homes, to international troubles and wars, we can see how intolerance is the underlying factor.

In between these two extremes of the purely personal and the worldwide effect, we find the same thing in business matters, sports, national and local government, religion as a whole, individual churches, a variety of organisations and charitable causes, and everyday procedures such as shopping, travelling and all manner of other daily activities. No-one escapes the frustrations and sorrows of another person's intolerance.

If only more tolerance were practised in all these fields of endeavour, so much suffering would be avoided – so much heartache.

And yet, the other side of the coin can be bothersome too. Should we for instance be tolerant towards other cultures in the world that cause suffering to both people and animals, in the mistaken belief that it is the right thing to do? They may be following many years of tradition or fighting for what they believe to be a just cause. But how can cruelty and suffering of any kind be considered a worthy situation of tolerance? Surely *in*tolerance is called for there. Many wonderful souls demonstrate the need for this type of intolerance by seeking to right the wrongs and reduce such suffering in practical ways, often at great risk to themselves. If tolerance towards the actions or habits of some, results in injury to health, minds or bodies of others, this can hardly be considered to be right or acceptable.

But how does one decide where and when to exercise tolerance, or when and how to exert some intolerance? Perhaps that well known guideline 'motive' is the true answer. If the intent is good, unselfish and spiritual, then either tolerance or its opposite side may be the correct attitude for action. But if the motive is selfish and has no consideration for other life, then it cannot be the right course.

In the end, we find as always, we have the freewill to choose between a right and wrong pathway, with only motive as our guide and that still small voice within, which brings us back to progression of the soul – our purpose for being here. The sensitive spirit that is learning well, begins to know the difference, and by example can lead the way for others to follow.

We can be in danger of falling into a trap of our own making, if we become impatient with those who do not understand our point of view. If we are not tolerant enough to those who fail to appreciate the value of this attribute, then we in our turn fail to show the way towards spiritual thinking – God's way. He in His mercy, depicts the epitome of tolerance. We can only try to follow that example and hope that others of less tolerant nature will follow ours. In this world we can only do our best, but maybe there are times when our own view of that, may not compare too well with the achievements we might accomplish if we tried just a little harder. Now we have gone full circle and are back to that still small voice within – that patient, tolerant guide that serves us all so well.

This particular piece is based on an article originally written for the Bideford Spiritualist Church magazine, and with the help of Spirit inspirers, was scribbled out in about ten minutes, using I noticed, a few words that would not normally come readily to my own mind. Under these circumstances I have to read what I have written before I *know* what I have written, and anyone who has experienced the same privilege of spirit guidance will understand the humble surprise that one feels on reading the results, for there always seems to be an angle that has not before been obvious. It is a very pleasant proof of the way that Spirit guides us, and uses every opportunity they can find to bring their truths to us. It is for us to recognise and use them well.

THE GIFT OF HEALING

If the Spiritual gifts of God could be evaluated and given an order of
precedence, then probably we mere mortals would place the gift of
healing on the throne of golden achievement. The actual facts give us a
wider picture, for although in earthly terms healing is the gift of which
we are most conscious and most appreciative, all the many gifts with
which we are endowed have their own special place and function. Each
one, used worthily and at the right time is fulfilling its function at that
moment, and is of greater value than any other gift used at the wrong
time or for the wrong purpose. The written or spoken word, the ability
to see, hear or sense spiritually – these and more all have their right
moments and purposes, when they can lift a soul to greater heights of
awareness, and are at that moment supreme. The healing gift can be a
part of all other gifts and yet stand alone in individuality. It is indeed a
pure and wonderful gift from God that passeth all understanding.

THE HEALING DAWN

The night time blessings greet the light
    Of every new born day.
The evening stars slip out of sight
    As blackbird stirs his lay.

A morning glow slips o'er the hill,
    To shine in bright array,
And all the world is hushed and still
    To greet the coming day.

With every morning born anew,
  Comes loving hope and healing.
The freshly falling morning dew,
  Perpetuates the gleaning.

The clarity of morning rays,
  Heals the soul that's torn
With sorrows of sad yesterdays,
  To shine again with dawn.

The passing of another day,
  Will cloud sad memories,
Bid them fade and fly away,
  With the healing dawn tomorrow.

THE SUPREME HEALING POWER

A healing thought that's tossed upon the air,
By a loving soul who knows the way to care,
Can drive away the darkness of despair
And by example, teach the way to share.

A healing prayer that flies to God supreme,
As flights of spirit angels bear the dream
Of loving hope, so peaceful and serene,
Returns to heal the soul and make it clean.

A healing love that knows no other course
But God, and His unfailing source
Of healing power, that perfect love endorse
To light the world – and all the universe.

A HEALING PRAYER

May the giving and receiving
Of God's own healing power,
Reveal to us the meaning
Of Spirit's timeless hour
Of peace and harmony within,
To ease the pain and sorrow,
May healing love this day begin,
Bring sweet content tomorrow.

★ ★ ★ ★ ★

THE HISTORY LESSON

It is strange how seemingly small unimportant events and situations
can have a profound influence upon a whole life or way of thinking,
and is not usually recognised until much later. One such memory in my
own life came about because of the history lessons I received at a
certain period, under the sharp eyes of my history teacher of that time.

I had moved to a different school, well known in the Ilford, Essex
area. On the whole I was quite happy there, although it was never able
to catch the affection I had held for the earlier school, Wanstead
College, which had closed and its pupils scattered into a harsh world.

Our history teacher was a large enthusiastic lady in every sense of
the word, with short, straight black hair which framed a round jovial
face and keen, piercing eyes. I can see her in my mind's eye even now,
some fifty years later. I recall a biting wit and sense of humour, and
most of all her taste for the blood and thunder parts of history. Miss K
revelled in the gory details of the torture chambers of the Tower of
London, the Spanish Inquisition, and all other tortuous records from
time immemorial.

On looking back, I do not doubt, that whilst satisfying her own taste for the horrific, she was convinced that the interest of her bunch of schoolgirls would be stimulated by the pictures of cruel suffering that she painted in the minds of her pupils. Perhaps she thought the agonised screams of the victims, were as much imagined music to *our* young ears as they were to her distorted older ones. Maybe some of the girls did enjoy this second hand horror and suffering, and perhaps the cause of history was well served by this degrading reflection of mankind, I cannot say. But I do know that Miss K completely destroyed any interest I might have had in the subject. I loathed the lessons, I cringed at her dark jokes and shuddered at the mental pictures she evoked.

Poor dear Miss K. How could she know there was a sensitive in her flock? I expect she was quite a kindly person really, but I couldn't see her that way at the time, and have no idea whether she would have been horrified herself at the effect she was having on me.

It is said that some good can come out of every situation if we will let it be so. I must admit now in retrospect, that those history lessons taught me quite a lot, even though it could hardly be classed as history.

They taught me not to dwell on the past and use it only as a lesson for the future. I learnt that man's inhumanity to all other life, has been a fault through all the ages of time, and that it is of primary importance to try to guide and teach against it. It is not possible for anyone to be sensitive to spiritual thinking, or the beautiful things of life, if such degradation exists within the mind and brain. The spark of glorious light that exists within each one of us, would not dare to show itself in such a dark place, for fear of being extinguished in the smothering blanket of evil that surrounds such thinking, and it is fortunate for us all that our inner light is protected in this way, no matter how we abuse it. Some people seem to actually enjoy the hurt, sorrow and pain that they inflict, see and hear around them. Only if such horrors are inflicted upon themselves do they cry out for mercy. Such is the law of cause and effect, such is the path that some choose to walk.

Until mankind can see the folly of this way of life and thinking, there must be those who suffer to learn and thereby learn to suffer. It means that there must still be those who wish to inflict that suffering, to enable others to pay their karmic debt, and in their own turn must suffer for the same reason. Clearly then, each soul that can be rescued from such desires before it goes too far, presents a positive step towards reduced suffering – a step towards a happier way of life for all. There are many other reasons why people suffer on this plane of life and circumstances alter with each individual, but the events quoted here serve to illustrate some angles which might not usually be considered.

Yes, my unhappy history lessons taught me quite a lot, although I am sure it was not exactly history as Miss K intended. Nevertheless, it was probably something I had to learn from experience, and Miss K was evidently used for the purpose. Her failure in one respect could turn to success in another, by the loving power of Spirit.

★ ★ ★ ★ ★

TODAY

Today is a very special day. It will last a mere twenty-four hours, has seen one beautiful sunrise and will see but one sunset, for this is all that one day is allowed. Yesterday it was an unknown quantity and quality of the future, tomorrow it will be history, maybe something worthwhile to remember, possibly something to recall with regret.

So many people seem to use so many of their todays delving into the past, regretting or glorying in it according to their circumstances, others look constantly to the future with thoughts and hopes and daydreams that may come true, but often don't. Meanwhile, today, that precious twenty-four hours that comes and goes so fleetingly, will have passed them by, and so little achievement to stand as recognition of a day well spent and worthy of a place in our personal history.

In our own short span of life on earth, it is such a pity that so many days are wasted, and only we who waste them are to blame, for even he who cannot move a limb can think, and he who thinks can pray, or lend his mind for Spirit to use to good purpose.

It is always important to maintain high hopes for the future, particularly when something appears to be going wrong today. It is also important to remember, that hope must be accompanied by thought and action for those hopes to be fulfilled.

When, at the end of the day we reflect on our achievements or the lack of them, it is wise not to be too bold in our own satisfaction, or too disappointed at failure. It may well be that we could have accomplished more had we tried a little harder, or that poor results were not so bad after all – success and failure are often difficult to assess when you are dealing with Spiritual matters rather than material ones. But it is important to create the right balance between using the past as guidance, using our God given common sense when looking at the future, and doing the very best we can with today – not merely for ourselves, although that must be considered too, but for everything and everybody that is part of that day, for they will be part of tomorrow, which will so quickly become 'today'.

Today is important because of the opportunities it gives us – perhaps only a kinder thought or word, maybe for a few a wondrous deed that will go down in the history of the world, but for most, the task of daily living in such a way that more will be accomplished to good purpose than the day before, tomorrow is for planning and dreaming. Yesterday is for guidance. Today is for living and action in the best way that we can. Today is a very special day.

THEIR MYSTERIOUS WAYS

At sometime in your life you will have looked back at some incident where plans appeared to go wrong. If you will allow memory to ring a bell for a moment, you may realise in retrospect that those plans did not go wrong at all, they in fact went right for you, although at the time it might have been an annoyance or even seemed to be a disaster, but by hindsight you realise it was the right way for you.

People find many and varied explanations for such phenomena – luck perhaps? premonition somewhere along the line? or was it an unseen guiding hand that steered the way? And if you thought this last was the explanation, did you pause in the rush of daily life to say "Thank you whoever you are"? Of course you might even have been aware of the identity of your helper – a few people are, not many – but sometimes the act carries the hallmark of someone in Spirit that you know so well that the situation is recognisable.

If you will let your memory ring another bell for a moment, you can probably think of many such incidents, and it is worthwhile to consider the implications of these occurrences in life, for they may have a much greater significance than you thought.

Many people have known a moment of sudden decision to cancel or postpone a journey, to discover afterwards that you would have been involved in an accident had your journey taken place. Alternatively, an incident at base, an unexpected visitor perhaps, may have given you cause to say, "Thank goodness I didn't go". Maybe some wonderful opportunity occurred for you because you did not make that journey.

Strange unexplained little happenings can occur which you feel must have some purpose, that is often revealed later – sometimes *much* later. That ambiguous word coincidence is often used as an explanation, but what in fact is coincidence? Merely an event or situation that seems to tie in with something else, but has no reason or logical explanation that you can find. For the most part such moments are dismissed, whereas it is often worthwhile to keep them in mind or investigate them further. The mind that is in tune with such things readily recognises the possibility of the hidden guiding hand.

Sometimes a coincidence can alert you to a situation you had not realised existed. There are times when it is a reminder of something you should remember but haven't. Several such signs occurring near to each other, can be a guidance for future action – a sort of tap on the shoulder to urge you on lest you allow an opportunity to pass by.

Often it conjures up a past memory of someone who wishes to let you know of their spiritual presence. The possibilities are endless, and once you are alerted to the significance of such fragments in the daily plan of things, a little practice can help you towards being an efficient coincidence spotter! It is a little bit like reading the signs of changes in the weather – if you know what to look for – the clues are there.

These clues are often used by those in Spirit who choose to guide and protect us. The warning against some proposed action on our own part is common. An encouragement towards a good situation is another. It is a favourite ploy to stimulate an interest in spiritual matters when an earthly soul is ready for progress and is instinctively beginning to search for such information. A train of unexpected events may lead you to a situation that is helpful in your search, or alternatively enable you to help someone else in *their* search.

I once had an acquaintance who missed a bus because of several unexpected delays. She walked into a nearby park to while away the half hour before the next bus would arrive. Sitting on a seat admiring the rose bed, she was joined by another lady and they began to talk. That lady was in deep sorrow from the loss of a husband. My bus-missing acquaintance with a rather limited knowledge of spiritual matters, nevertheless knew enough to start the widowed lady on a happier way of thinking by explaining certain strange happenings in her home as the efforts of the recently passed husband trying to make his presence felt. His wife was overjoyed at this revelation and profoundly expressed her thanks for the enlightenment. Meanwhile the next bus was caught just in time and the journey gave an opportunity for reflection on the happy coincidences that led to the missing of the first bus and the idle wander into the park – at the right time! These facts helped to substantiate her own growing awareness.

When full consideration is given to the amount of planning, manipulation and careful thought that is required to bring about such a result, one can only marvel at the skills and patience of those in Spirit who organise such things. What a joy it must be to them when their object is achieved, how disappointing when their efforts fall upon deaf ears and fail. It must happen only too often.

There is virtually no end to the ways in which our spirit friends can protect, guide and help us if we are willing to respond. Some years ago, whilst sitting in meditation, I saw a beautiful rainbow against a clear blue background, the strange thing about the rainbow was that it was made of flowers. I made a written note of it at the time, but it was much later on that I realised it was the cover of our first book, Kaleidoscope Of Living Thoughts. In the event, we were unable to use the rainbow colours, but the arch of flowers remained as a very attractive and symbolic cover for the book.

The cover for our second book, I'm Jane, came about because our friend Anne sent me a delightful birthday card that so fascinated me that I kept it and used it to decorate our folder of Spirit drawings. Several years later, I awoke one morning with that picture very clearly in my mind, although I had not recently used the folder. I just knew that I was to use it as the basis for the cover of I'm Jane, and indeed it perfectly conveyed the fay quality of her story.

The picture for the cover of Memory Rings The Bells, is based on a scribbled drawing that I committed to paper after seeing it mentally as we 'sat' together in the silence of our Rainbow Room. Such moments seem to spring from nowhere and can easily take us unawares, but experience soon teaches us to recognise a spirit message in whatever form it takes – providing we are willing and have learnt the art of humble acceptance. I am reminded now that the titles of all three books came to me under similar circumstances to the covers – memory rings the bells yet again!

We upon the earthplane make so much confusion by hastily flitting from one thing to another, that we do not create the placid frame of mind that can recognise the clues we are given, still less give ourselves time to act upon them. And yet these helpers in the world of spirit patiently persevere in their self-allotted task of helping us, by being instruments for the work of God, just as we too upon the earthplane can also serve His master plan.

The mysterious ways of Spirit will remain so until we are also in that privileged world where we can learn and give service in the same rewarding way, thereby making progression for our own souls automatically.

Meanwhile, our task on earth is made the easier by listening to the voice of spirit guidance which speaks to us in such mysterious and unexpected ways.

AN ORGAN ACCOMPANIMENT

I was playing the organ for a service at Christchurch Spiritualist Church, when words came into my head that were different from the ones the congregation were singing!

As soon as the last note of the hymn had faded away, and shielded from the congregation by the organ, I hastily began scribbling, and in a very few minutes produced the following hymn. It is in the metre of 8686D and can be sung to the tune Ellacombe.

No doubt the atmosphere and vibrations in the church that evening were helpful to spirit communication, as the words themselves suggest – further evidence to demonstrate the willingness of Spirit beings to use every opportunity to contact and help us on the earthplane. Who else would produce one hymn whilst another was being sung! Who else would work in such a mysterious way?

> The love that guides us day by day,
> Still guards us through each night,
> And when we walk the Spirit way,
> God makes our darkness light.
> The gentle love just leads us on,
> And soothes the lonely heart,
> For truth will dawn on everyone
> Who seeks the veil to part.
>
> Just sing the songs of truth and love,
> That all around may hear,
> Welcome the souls from heaven above
> Who seek to draw so near.
> The love they bring is pure and true,
> And from their light will shine
> A brightness that is strong and new
> Yet old as God's own time.

A WELCOME FOR SPIRIT FRIENDS

Who would deny the right of loved ones in Spirit to come to us, help us, laugh with us and cry with us just as they did on earth? Who are we to say they cannot come to cheer and guide us? What right have we to say they must not come? Yet many folk upon our earthplane do just that.

We cannot demand their presence, it is for them to choose. But if their objects are sincere and our own motives are right, then there can be wondrous experience, and much love expressed between those that have always loved. Such things could not happen without God's blessing, for man knows not how it happens or how it can be accomplished. It is therefore beyond our understanding, and so must be from the greater knowledge of Spirit.

That knowledge sees the wider view, understands our hopes and fears, only aims to help us all, so that with heart and mind we may benefit from that superior knowledge, and become conscious of the love it bears.

By our own acceptance, we acknowledge that love, and open the door to the wonder that Spirit offers, as they work for us in their own mysterious ways.

A ROAD TO HEAVEN

Silently he walked the miles,
    Lonely and misunderstood,
Scarcely could he climb the hill,
    Tired and weak through lack of food.

In his hand he held a life,
    Abandoned by another man,
Pleading eyes no longer bright,
    Gazed from the puppy in his hand.

And then a lady saw his plight,
    She gave him sustenance,
He smiled his thanks with sheer delight,
    And fed the life he'd found by chance.

Strengthened now his way he trod
   Along the winding road,
Towards the love that he called God,
   That He might share his load.

The lady hurried after him,
   A tear slipped from her eye,
This man in lonely wandering,
   Had shared without a sigh.

"Come back" she said "and I will find
   Some food for you as well".
"My lady you are very kind –
   May this baby with you dwell?"

She took the puppy to her heart,
   For she was lonely too.
The gentle stroke 'ere he depart,
   For the life that was so new.

And so three lives brushed quietly,
   Like ships that pass at night.
A puppy now with home and love,
   And two memories shining bright.

The mysteries of Spirit's plans,
   The trails of chance encounters,
Are there for loving helping hands
   To use all God's endeavours.

And when all earthly life is done,
   And each has played their part,
The glory that each soul has won,
   Depends on a kindly heart.

APRIL GARDEN

The primrose shyly peeping now
Beneath the fern fronds curve unfurled.
April violets scent the airflow,
Amongst the hedgerow leaves uncurled.

The glinting gold of daffodils
Puts to shame the miser's hoard.
Springtime's promise still fulfills
The prayer of souls throughout the world.

For nature's circle of all life,
Continues on with April's choir,
Puts in tune the world of strife,
And orchestrates the sunrise fire.

This morning chorus blends and lilts
Amongst the hopeful budding trees,
When April breezes sway and tilt
Young branches, shaking out their leaves.

And so the garden now reflects
The shining hopes of yester-year,
The glimpse that nature now expects,
Of future joy and beauty near.

NOT A SPARROW SHALL FALL

It was in the month of April 1958 that I came to one of those milestones in life whose importance we usually do not understand until much later. This particular milestone appeared when I began working at the People's Dispensary for Sick Animals.

My office was at their Technical Headquarters at Ilford in Essex, and it was here that all major operations for the area were carried out. In those days, a P.D.S.A. hospital was surrounded by smaller clinics, over which the hospital presided like a mother hen with a brood of chicks. It naturally followed that the Head Surgeon was an important person.

I remember an occasion only about one week after my appearance at the "Sanatorium" as it was affectionately known, when I was so immeasurably impressed that it has stayed vividly with me ever since.

It was lunchtime, and I discovered the Head Surgeon – no less – with the Radiologist, also of some considerable importance, carrying a very old heavy fire ladder across the grounds to a building next to my office. This picturesque sixteenth century home was the St. Swithin's Farm mentioned in Charles Dicken's "Barnaby Rudge", and was covered in the most beautiful wisteria I have ever seen. These two important personages raised the heavy ladder to the eaves in order to replace a tiny, almost naked sparrow in its nest. I well remember the dozens of nests that had been built in the shelter of that wisteria and the ancient eaves of the farmhouse, and I well remember too the hand of Mr. White the surgeon, opening to show me this tiny victim of some birdy accident or crime. I thought how wonderful it was that these two men should use their lunch break to give this help and comfort to such a tiny scrap of life. This humane act by Mr. White and Mr. Chubb set for me a pattern of the work and ideals of the place that never left me in the whole twenty years that I remained there.

Many years later, I was attending the funeral of that same Mr. White at far away Boldre Church in Hampshire, when another experience occurred that will also remain with me – yet such a small occurrence.

The church service was over, and Mr. White's many friends, relations and colleagues were walking away from the grave. The grave-diggers were standing respectfully aside until all had gone from sight. It was so still and quiet in that beautiful little New Forest churchyard, and I paused as I left the now lonely looking mounds of earth that waited in the silence to be returned from whence they came. A sparrow suddenly appeared on the peak of the highest mound of soil, and standing there peered towards the hole in the ground that now contained the earthly remains of that kindly man. Fascinated, I watched as the bird raised its head and loudly cheeped the funny little song that only sparrows know. I could have wept just then to see this tiny, ordinary little bird that seemed to me to be paying last respects to a great man who so many years before had saved a tiny helpless sparrow, using precious relaxation time amongst the pressure of his daily work. A few brief moments in three different lives (the surgeon's, the sparrow's and mine) had come together so long ago, made an impression that would be imprinted in the history book of heaven, and here was its moment of recognition.

It was a fitting salutation that only I could have appreciated, for only I saw the fledgling in his hand, and only I saw and heard the requiem another sparrow sang. Perhaps not – I like to think the surgeon saw it too.

★ ★ ★ ★ ★

PETS IN MY LIFE

It has been my privilege to own and be owned, by a number of animals during my lifetime, and all have taught me well, lessons of one kind and another. All have had something special to give me, and gave unstintingly. I hope my own gifts of love and care to them were sufficient "thank you", I think they were, because part of the charm of pets is that they ask so little in return for their love and loyalty to us. Not from them a sullen frown if we have spoken sharply, nor sulky silence if we have been out without them. And if they do display these things, it's with a twinkle in the eye, preceding a late welcome – just to tease us.

Inevitably some pets seem to find a special niche within our hearts and minds, and usually it would be difficult to explain the reason. One of mine is an Alsatian German Shepherd – Judy. Gentle as a loving touch, but strong and firm according to the need – as she saw it. She collected eggs and wandering day-old chicks without harm or damage, and held a burly six foot intruder at bay, also without damage, although I fear he felt a little nervous and wished he hadn't come. Not only did she guard me, but she sympathised when I was sad, or jumped for joy when I was glad. She displayed a mischievous sense of humour when she felt like it, and showed a remarkable intelligence and power of reasoning.

I recall the day she danced a sort of canine polka in her attempts to draw a young lodger's attention to the fact that she had left her new baby in his pram outside a shop in the village, some 500 yards or more up the road! And another occasion when she rushed into the kitchen anxiously persuading me to go out to the garden – to find the same baby, then about 18 months old – leaning and peering dangerously into a deep pond, watching the goldfish. I dared not startle him, and Judy had the good sense to stand back and wait for me to draw him away from danger with a quiet call, before dashing to the pond and placing herself between it and the baby. Such thought and action by a dog challenges the theory to its very roots that animals cannot reason, and demonstrates yet again the way that spirit helpers can use both us and animals towards helping each other. Animals, and perhaps domestic ones especially, are nearly always psychic to some degree, some more than others just as it varies in us humans, who share this world – and the next – with them. Mediums have seen Judy with me several times since her passing, and that certainly doesn't surprise me.

Tina on the other hand, is a lively Yorkshire Terrier, now in Spirit, who also found a special place for many different reasons. She always seemed aware of the times when I was sitting for distant healing, although these sittings were not at regular times at that period of my life. She always seemed to know, and would appear from nowhere, sit bolt upright on my lap until the session was over, and I always felt she was helping in some way. She too displayed a saucy sense of humour, and particularly enjoyed indulging in twisting contortions on the sofa whilst having her harness put on, until you couldn't tell which end of the dog was which, for it was just a whirling bundle of fur and legs. She would suddenly stop and survey you with twinkley eyes, that clearly said "Did you enjoy that? I did!" Only then could you fasten the harness. Anyone who has been owned by a Yorkshire Terrier will know what I mean, and I am sure there are many other kinds of dogs with similar traits, the ones that you love so much that just to look at them gives your heart a lurch sometimes – the ones that in the fullness of their mischief, can make you want to laugh – and box their ears (with a feather duster) all at the same time!

Four days after Tina passed to spirit, I received this Spirit inspired poem, which I share with you here in the hope that it will help another pet owner. Little One as I often called her, would I think be pleased, as she always shared her happy little self with everyone.

TINA

A little soul came here to earth,
   To share her loyal doggie love.
She came and suffered earthly birth,
   Gentle as the peaceful dove.

Yet gaiety and joy she brought,
   Mischief twinkling in her eyes,
To share with humans who had sought
   Upliftment with their lonely sighs.

She who watched her spirit friends
   Moving silently around,
Knew the harmony that blends
   The psychic with the earthly sound.

Patience was the lesson brought,
   And timeless joy in simple things.
Tolerance the gift she taught
   To us who are mere human beings.

An understanding sympathy,
   When others failed to know,
A whispering of telepathy,
   Quick lick on unsuspecting nose!

Yet fun and games were also part
   Of Tina's willing life,
Courageous little doggy heart
   Was lent for our delight.

With ears pricked up and eyes ashine,
   "We're going out I think,
That harness there, I know is mine,
   We'll be ready in a wink".

But first there's something she must do,
   Expressing her delight –
Bouncing, wriggling joys anew,
   The sofa springs just right.

So many were the joys she gave,
   In the twinkling of an eye,
Heart warming in her Yorkie way,
   Remembered with a sigh.

This little life so blest with love,
   And strength of personality,
Returning to her home above,
   Life lent in true simplicity.

She asked so little, gave so much,
   But now her earthly task is done,
I know she's well, but miss her touch,
   God Bless your soul, my Little One.

I've heard it said that we humans shouldn't keep pets, that we make them so dependent upon us, that they become our slaves. If we do, then they are very willing, happy slaves, and I have a sneaky feeling that it is more likely that *we* are willing slaves to *them*. Either way, it is an exchange of loving affection and loyalty that serves as a very worthwhile example to those who know too little about these things, and our world would surely be a better place if we had more of them.

In any case, the domestication of animals by man started too many years ago for us present-day inhabitants of the earth to be able to alter the situation between pets and their owners. You cannot undo what has been done, and through the years mankind has taken animals into his home and heart, thereby bringing them nearer to human habits and thinking. We are fortunate that they have not also picked up our more debased thoughts and actions. Let us hope they never do so. Meanwhile their nearness to us, by our own design, enables them to be spiritually more advanced than their wild counterparts.

Having done that, who are we to deny them now continued opportunities for progression? Mankind has written the story, printed the script, produced the play and cast the actors in it, and we are committed to the performances that are acted out day after day in millions of homes throughout the world. The animals are here with us, helping us as we help them, and this particular avenue of evolution must now go on, each helping the other. There is no turning back. At the moment the balance falls heavily on our side of the scale, and we who truly care about animals must do our part to create a better balance.

Our current niche makers, are a tiny pair of Yorkshire Terriers, half the size of their predecessor, but certainly not with half the quantity of character. Seventeen months old at the time of writing in 1988, they have had a fairly rough passage healthwise, and we realise they were meant to come to us for all the extra time and care we are able to give them in our retirement, which many other people could not have done. Not everyone has a really deep understanding of an animal's needs, and we feel we are able to give them that little extra help and consideration that they so obviously need. Other people will have a greater knowledge in other fields of endeavour and service, but just now, our thoughts are with animals.

Poppette dashes enthusiastically about in spite of a foreleg in plaster, since she broke it in a miscalculated jump from the car more than ten weeks ago. It does not heal as it should in spite of all our efforts, but she seems to have enough courage for four, as her twinkling eyes peering through the furry curtain that shades them, tell of determination and fun. If only we could all summon up such a spirit in the face of adversity – a big and obvious lesson from a tiny bundle of loving furry life.

Her companion Daisy, is a beauty of her breed, and is obviously well aware of it, although delighting in looking as untidy as possible. At nine weeks she suffered a severe attack of bronchial pneumonia, and it almost seemed that her stay with us would be very short indeed. But thanks to the attentions of our Veterinary Surgeon, the special care we were able to give her, and above all the healing from our Spirit friends, she is happily with us still, getting strong and twice the weight of Poppette. She ignores her own toys for the most part, and quietly and determinedly 'whips up' any small objects that take her fancy. Pencils, pens, rubbers, an eye glass, small plastic containers, socks and slippers, all prove to be of great interest, though rarely harmed. She is like the small child who prefers mum's saucepans to his own building bricks. These constant demonstrations of pets and children thinking and behaving in similar ways, must surely have a lesson for us all in the way we should treat our pets, and in some cases, perhaps the way we should treat our children.

This jolly little pair came to us when we had scoured the area for a Yorkie puppy in vain, until Poppette came into view because her new would-be owners were army people who had suddenly been posted abroad and therefore had to cancel. She was literally the only one available at that time throughout two counties. I recognised her immediately as a "Betty puppy" – one that was meant for me. All my pets, including some lovely character cats, have come via circumstances that suggest an unseen guiding hand. Some of our readers will have experienced the same knowledge of an 'It had to be' situation. Daisy came almost as an after-thought from the same kennels but eleven days later, being that much younger. The lady who bred her had shown us this second puppy at the time we went to fetch Poppette. The way she snuggled into Ken's neck and gently cooed, then fell asleep, well – we were of course caught in the tender trap, and collected her two weeks later. Lots of people will recognise that situation!

They already knew every heart tugging trick there is, their fluffy heads turning from side to side as they peered at you with sparkling eyes. Those funny little button noses and their rolling gait, their tiny outstretched paws towards a passing butterfly and their stalking of an invading garden beetle across the carpet – it might have been a dragon! Goodness me, we didn't stand a chance. Their comic games and childlike puppy reasoning brought forth laughter and amazement in us both. We were back to normal after Tina's passing a few months previously.

The roll-over-on-the-back technique, the furry paws waving in the air, was a complete sellout, promoting in us, the one-finger – tummy-tickle urge which cannot be denied. If you could keep it up long enough – and it wasn't difficult – they would close those twinkley eyes and go to sleep in the same upturned position. Poppette in particular was prone to this delight – and still is; and have you ever been "attacked" by a teddy bear? It's great fun!

We know that the animal psychologists have adequate explanations for all this sort of behaviour, the scientific mind can find flat scientific reasons for almost anything, but as far as we are concerned, we are not bothered about why our pets do these things – sufficient that they do them, they delight us in the process and create much happiness around them. We can certainly do with more of that.

Many instances come to our notice of that unseen guiding hand working to help us through an animal, and equally, using us mere humans to help an animal. This balance is needed in all aspects of life, and in this case demonstrating the special relationship that exists between so many people and their pets.

THE MANY FACES OF FEAR

The following piece was written on 6th October, 1988, the first part being based on a trance communication received in April 1985 (and later written out) from our own Communicator "Friend" whom we knew by his voice. The handwriting then changed and the remainder given by someone else in Spirit, although no indication was given about the actual inspirer. It is of interest to note that those in Spirit who seek to guide and help us attach little importance to the name of the communicator – sufficient for them that their message is received by us with the opportunity to benefit thereby.

Consider carefully the two aspects of fear – the positive and the negative. The positive protects and even creates under some circumstances, but the negative reduces and can destroy.

Negative thinking never helps in any situation. When related to fear it can have all kinds of undesirable results, for it twists the thinking and produces dishonest thought and action. It causes people to utter untrue words in order to protect themselves from some approaching calamity. It creates unkind or even cruel action towards others, lest the perpetrator be engulfed himself in such action from associates, whether they be a recognised foe or someone masquerading as a friend.

Fear can destroy not only the one who feels this fear and experiences the horror of it, but also can affect people around that person, who may be in direct line to receive the consequences of it, or maybe just on the sidelines of the situation. Friends or relations are often on the edge of fear prompted conditions and experience fear themselves, either for that friend or relative or for themselves. It is such a powerful emotion which may be experienced to any degree, that its mere thought transference ability makes it a very potent destroyer of peace. Those engaged in any kind of dishonesty are always in fear of being found out for instance. It spreads to others who may not even be aware of the cause, and like a dark canker spoils much fruit of good thinking.

Yet positive fear protects and guides. It triggers flight or defence in a dangerous situation by a chemical reaction in the body. It alerts to undesirable conditions and cushions the soul and the mind against adverse resulting effects.

The positive value of fear is easily seen amongst animals in the wild, where a whole herd of animals becomes conscious of danger from another species, and fear will trigger flight or fight according to their natural habit. To a lesser degree it can also be observed in domesticated animals. A cat for instance may spit at an adversary, or lash out with extended claws. A different cat would take cover and hide until danger is past. A blackbird on finding a cat nearby will not only fly to safety, but give an alarm call that is recognised by other birds. All these reactions are prompted by a natural and positive fear that is designed to protect.

People react to potential dangers by natural positive fear, and it is unfortunate that it is sometimes considered to be degrading, and a person may be judged to be behaving in a cowardly way in the face of danger.

The first point here is that one person should never judge another. One needs to assess from time to time in order to live in earthplane conditions, but judgement is another matter because all the relevant facts cannot be known unless viewed from the greater knowledge of Spirit. People for example vary in their ability to withstand pain of either the body or mind. Some more sensitive persons will have known pain of the soul, but that is another matter and does not come into considerations of the emotion fear.

Fear can also be tempered by knowledge. A strong swimmer might experience little fear if contemplating the rescue of a drowning person, whereas a weak swimmer would have to overcome considerable fear in order to attempt it. This brings us to the subject of bravery. It can safely be said that the person who overcomes strong feelings of fear in order to take action on someone else's behalf is exhibiting greater bravery than the one who knows little fear. But as no-one else can know the extent of these personal inner feelings of fear, it is not possible for a fellow being to assess the difference, and this is one basic reason why judgement cannot be made of a fellow human being on the earthplane. Knowledge and understanding of that knowledge will always help to reduce fear, simply because it aids in assessing a situation and any action that may be required, the risks and potential success or failure.

Many brave deeds occur in times of stress, such as fires, shipwrecks and wars. These actions of extreme bravery are sometimes made by persons who would normally not be thought of in this way. Often they say afterwards that they didn't feel any fear at the time, they just acted. This is because their inner knowledge of finer and Spiritual thinking has come to the surface in time of need. It could even be an inner knowledge of the soul from a past life, but whatever the reason their more evolved inner self enables Spirit to come to their aid in time of extreme need, quelling their natural fear and at the same time protecting them. Once again, no earthly person would be in a position to know these things.

Nervous reaction, a form of fear often experienced by someone doing something unusual for them, happens so often that such occasions go unnoticed for the most part. The perfectionist will experience a greater sensation of 'nerves' under these circumstances than one who feels less responsibility to reach perfection. The fear of failure in this case is a positive fear that will create greater success. The person's own ability to overcome his or her own fears will be a positive step forward to give confidence at future similar occasions.

It is during an occasion that requires courage that negative fear may enter and cause a chaotic situation. New factors may suddenly become apparent and give an added test of the courage, or the positive thinking may simply be not strong enough to complete the task. Either way, a request for help from Spirit will not go unanswered, a prayer if you like, and it happens countless times. Too few think to offer thanks afterwards for the help received to overcome the fear that prompted the appeal.

Most people instinctively know that unseen help is available. Even those without any belief or knowledge of God or Spiritual matters will cry out for help in extreme fear, thus exhibiting an inner knowledge – an inner knowledge which they did not realise they had, or had perhaps previously denied. This situation demonstrates the ability of fear to teach, and trigger a new awareness of Spirit.

The greatest universal fear upon the earthplane is the fear of death, and this my friends is the one thing of which you need have no fear.

If you come to us in the world of Spirit with kindness and love in your heart, if you have tried your best to live a good life within the laws of God – no matter what label you had for your beliefs or the lack of them – then you will be welcomed by many, including those you have loved on earth and those who have loved you and still do. You will rest a little while according to the needs of your mind and spirit, not your physical body which will no longer concern you. Here you will find all the wonder and love you could ever hope for, all the beauty that you have ever envisaged and far more. Your loved ones will share all this with you, and you will experience the nearest to perfection that you have ever dreamt of.

If your earth life was of a low spiritual standard, you will still be met by those who love you, and you will be helped to greater understanding if this is what you wish. You will need longer to acclimatise to your different conditions, but in the end you will reach the same delightful state as anybody else. Only your own desire to progress or otherwise dictates the time it takes.

If you happen to be one who has lived what one might term an actual evil life on the earthplane, even if no-one else was able to come to you on passing to Spirit, your own personal guide would greet and help you, the one who has lovingly tried to help you all through your earth life. That guide, whilst sorrowing at your lack of progress, will also be joyful that further closer attempts can be made to assist you to a higher plane of thinking, which you will do in due course according to your own wishes, and that guide will always be able to help you. No, nobody need ever fear the condition known as death.

Many who already have this knowledge still fear the process of dying. They need not do so. If a soul is taken suddenly by violence or accident, the guides will know of this before it occurs, and will assist the spirit from the earthly body as quickly as is necessary. Many have testified to this experience, and explained how, after such a sudden passing, they have stood by or perhaps above their own earthly body and actually watched proceedings for a short while until taken away by the Spirit helpers. They usually make a point of saying that they cannot remember any feeling of pain, and their only recollection is one of freedom.

Those of you who appear to suffer pain in terminal illness have occasionally chosen to do so yourselves – perhaps for a Karmic purpose, perhaps to learn something for future use. More often in such cases the spirit has in fact partly left the body. The apparent suffering is more in keeping with an instinctive reaction associated with the physical nervous system, and is not a true expression of the experience. If pain is felt at this time, the reasons are not different from the reasons for pain at any other time on the earthplane. Therefore it is clear that you do not need to fear dying any more than you need to fear pain at any other time. So often it is but to close the eyes and go to sleep, to awaken in a pain-free world of peace and beauty. Whatever the circumstances, you will always be helped and supported. It is often those whose task it is to watch a loved one apparently in pain, who need even greater help to bear the situation. For those too, help and understanding is there for the asking.

And so you can see how complex is the subject of fear. It is perhaps the most noxious emotion on the earthplane when exhibited in its negative form, which is the only one that really needs to be feared. Never fear positive fear, it protects and guides you and can be used by your spirit guides and helpers to good purpose, and this is something for which to be truly thankful.

★ ★ ★ ★ ★

SUMMER IS ON IT'S WAY

The hush that heralds summer's sultry day,
Hovers in the air not far away.
The gentle rains that fall begin to say,
Summer flowers will bloom with bright array.

Nesting birds have flitted to and fro,
Fluttering offspring follow where they go.
Nature now will leap to summer's glow,
The Master plan dictates it will be so.

Anticipation of the summer sun,
Long days of toil and happy joyful fun,
With summer flowers and fruit for everyone,
Demands a prayer of thanks when day is done.

Blest are the sounds of summer's golden ray,
As birdsong greets another newborn day
Lambs will run and gambol in their play,
And we will know that summer's on its way.

THE POWER OF RIGHT THINKING

On 22nd April, 1987, at 7.00 am, the following was received through trance mediumship, from our Communicator of spiritual philosophy, known to us merely as "Friend".

There is much reference throughout your world to the forces of evil and wickedness. It has been so throughout the ages of mankind, and his experiences upon the earthplane. Since the beginning of time for man, dreadful things have been perpetrated in the name of evil and wickedness, until today it is thought of in an objective way as if it were an actual living thing, drifting around the world, uncontrollable by man, and affecting his thought and action without his permission. This is not so. Mankind is the only inhabitant of the earthplane that is subject to the thoughts and actions of evil and wickedness.

The animal life which inhabits the earth does not deliberately perpetrate cruel and wicked acts on others for the sake of their own advancement in their environment. The material advancement that the animal world can have is dependent upon the actions of man, and man has fallen very short in this respect. Indeed his thoughts and actions push the animal kingdom into a disadvantageous position.

The evils of the world, the sufferings perpetrated by man, come purely from the mind of man. Truly it is an evil force. But evil is not a power brought about by some god of darkness in opposition to the Great Spirit, who brings about good thought, charitable thought, kindness and love. There is no god of evil as such, it is a power conjured up by mankind himself, and only he can dispel it and defeat it. The God of Love will help mankind to overcome this tremendous problem. The power of the Great Loving God is infinite and can easily overcome these darker forces, but mankind must wish it to be so. All over your world there are isolated spots, where perhaps one, perhaps a hundred or more people are gathered, who work towards this end, to dispel the hatred and the cruelty that is inflicted on others.

This band of thinking power grows gradually but forcefully, eventually the results will be seen more positively than now, and those who work in this way for good need not be disappointed at the apparent evils around them. True, they are there, but their power decreases with every increase of thought of love, every increase of thought of compassion. If those who love peace, those who understand the loving compassion of God that has influenced them and can influence others – if those people would but realise the power they send forth, the power that can be collected, and help others upon a like course, then they would not despair, they would continue and increase their efforts to help and influence others of dark thinking.

These others who are not interested in compassion and love towards their fellow man, can only be influenced by example, for they will not change until they wish to change. But by the example of kindly people and the power of their loving thoughts, so an atmosphere will be created that will help many of these poor sorrowing souls to feel the need for improvement within themselves. We speak of the darkness of the mind, for the mind that is filled with evil thought is dark. The mind that is filled with love and compassion is bright. It is so bright that we can see these lights through the darkness of the world's atmosphere. And so we ask that those who understand this need, will make even greater effort and be assured of the loving help and guidance from Spirit, because although each personal effort may seem too small for any significant effect, always remember that every mighty mountain is but a vast collection of tiny grains of sand – various kinds of sand, as indeed are the efforts of the individual person upon the earth plane.

THE MAGIC BLACKBIRD

I hear you magic blackbird
   From your blossomed bough,
My sleek and lovely songbird,
   Your trills are praises now,
That lift towards your maker
   In gratitude for life,
And nature's own creator
   Accepts your song of love.

I see you magic blackbird
   Defend your territory,
I watch you lovely songbird
   Rise up with majesty,
For the younger life that follows
   Under your protecting wing,
Will also know the sorrows
   That life on earth can bring.

I love you magic blackbird,
   Your courage is supreme,
I'll tell you lovely songbird,
   Of my secret dream.
I'd fly with you to heaven,
   Singing all the way,
That man finds God is proven,
   And God may hear me pray.

The lines of the foregoing poem came spasmodically over a period of
two days in April, 1989. Many of us have known our own private

blackbirds at various times in our lives – the one that will sit on the windowsill and tap on the glass, or the one with a damaged wing or leg that calls upon our sympathy and some extra and easily found food. Maybe one appears with a blind eye or white feathers amongst its plumage. Often one particular bird will use a specially chosen tree or shrub in our garden as its own stage setting for its vocal performance, and we feel privileged. We may be honoured with a blackbird's nest in our own garden and feel a personal interest towards it and its baby contents. We share with our blackbird the fear of a magpie or neighbour's cat that is yet to develop the kinder approach to birds and other small wild creatures. We admire the tenacity that our blackbird displays in defence of home and young, and on occasion try to lend a helping hand, usually to little avail, the birds invariably know best just what to do.

Our own special blackbird nested in one of our conifers, and he chose a small weeping cherry as his song post. There he lifted his music above all other sounds, mostly it seemed in exhilaration of joyful springtime, until a melancholy note crept in, the pace slackened, for his nest had been robbed. The battle had raged – on and off – through most of the day, as the pair of magpies broke into this tiny stately home, and one by one robbed the parents of their eggs that soon would have been new young life to sing, and beguile other human beings.

We tried to help, and our blackbird friends defended bravely, even attacking the larger birds in defence of home and family – their only worldly possessions. It was all to no avail and our songbirds had to begin their family planning all over again.

Perhaps our shining, singing friends offer us an example we could all follow with advantage. Would some of us for example, be happier with fewer worldly possessions? Concentrating on actual needs rather than idle wants?. Could we have more courage in defence of those important things that are rightly ours – the natural things around us, the freedom to think and worship God in our own way? Perhaps we have the right even to attack in self defence and the preservation of these things and weaker lives that depend upon us. Some would not agree, but our blackbird did, and in doing so, lived to sing for us, start again and provide another family to sing the joys of living in their own turn, even though the first battle had been lost. His determination ensured the continuation of one tiny part of God's own plan.

Individually we are so small, yet we each have an important part to play in the evolution of life and time. Our own small blackbird, now immortalised in verse and printed word, will catch another eye and ear for many years to come – enhance another mind and heart, give courage where it otherwise might fail. It demonstrates the gentle move forward of Spirit's plans, evolving, dovetailing into those things that are good, and when the earthly lives of he and I are long since gone, maybe we shall sing in harmony together in a happy spirit home, for who on earth can prove it to be otherwise?

Some people, like the magpies seem to live at the expense of others, but while the blackbirds of human life continue to defend and bravely fight for what is right with a song in their hearts, then right will always prevail, for the balance of nature deems it must be so. The laws of nature are God's laws and we are the tools and instruments by which His laws are carried out. It is for us to choose whether we are the magpies, handsome though they may be, with their greed and callousness, or the blackbirds with their courage and their magic song.

MAY GARDEN

The month of May – she charms us still,
The bright fresh days will yet fulfil
Our hopes of sunshine's warming thrill,
And the soaring skylark's joyous trill,
For summer is nearly here.

The vegetable plots are green,
With promise for the harvest scene
Of beet and carrot and runner bean,
And sunrise gleams with silver sheen,
For summer's almost here.

The hawthorn proudly now displays
Her scented dress of bygone days,
Renewed again by nature's ways,
And hides the fledgling as she plays,
And knows that summer's here.

Bluebells nod their graceful heads,
Hyacinths rise from well planned beds,
And lawnmowers trundle from their sheds
To neaten where a lady treads,
Now that summer's here.

The joyous sound of birds in tune,
Mingle with the rich perfume
Of pinks and lilac in full bloom,
Thrilling the air and gone too soon,
For summer is truly here.

Hope is high in the month of May,
Some glory has been – yet passed away,
But there's much more for a later day.
So lift your thoughts to God and pray,
With thanks that May is here.

★ ★ ★ ★ ★

REFLECTIONS ON FRIENDSHIP

Ever since I first experienced the desire to write, being unaware at the time of the inspirational and spiritual elements involved, I have written short articles and verses on the subject of friendship. Some of these have been for special friends or occasions, others are of a more general nature as my fancy or humour took me. Certain poems appear elsewhere in this book, being relevant to the specific subject to which they are attached. Others I have gathered together under this heading of Reflections, in the hope that our readers will find comfort, upliftment or food for thought as the case may be – for them. For me, my friends have always been important to me, for I have learnt from them whilst hopefully they have learnt something useful from me, for what is this life if it's ebb and flow of friendships do not sometimes wash a treasure onto our own personal beach. When it comes, sometimes amongst the flotsam and jetsam of our lives, it is a precious gem that puts the finest diamond into dull obscurity. It trusts and is trusted, it loves and is loved, it gives and it takes with equal honesty, and shares it's ups and downs of life with true impartiality. It is a rare flower in true perfection, and while the species defies extinction – as it does – we who nurture it and prize its habitat, can still gaze in wonder at the miracle of friendship – a gift from God.

Friendship means different things to different people, and it is possibly one of the most abused words in the many languages of the world, for many treat their friends as acquaintances while others pretend their acquaintances are friends.

While some people give their all in friendship, others take all in its noble name and stain the word with selfishness, dishonesty, a kind of moral blackmail or mere neglect. History tells of those who plot and scheme whilst disguised in cloaks of friendship even unto death for those whose trust they have betrayed. Yet through it all, sincere friendship survives the traps and tricks of sheer betrayal of any kind, as demonstrated often through turbulent times past, and shines ever brighter in its truth by contrast with the darkness of the false and treacherous.

Some friendships last a lifetime, surmounting many difficulties along the way that serve to strengthen, whilst others are as brief as ships that pass each other in the night, yet during that brief encounter, forge a bond that stays in memory for all time.

Childhood friendships come and go and can be trivial or intense according to the nature of them and the children involved. But certainly they will be tossed to and fro, blow hot and cold, die a thousand deaths but usually survive the unthinking maltreatment of the very young, and the memories can sometimes stay through life. Some adults barely grow out of this adolescent type of friendship, and fail to realise that such a partnership should mature with its own increasing span and knowledge. Such souls may never know the wonder of true and lasting friendship – to their loss.

Some friendships – like some marriages – appear to have been made in heaven. Perhaps they have; maybe two souls planned to meet on earth and work together there in some way, their strengths and weaknesses balancing out into a perfect partnership. They could be born into the same family, or seek each other to marry, or perhaps find unlikely circumstances bringing them together on parallel paths in some respects, whilst deviating slightly in others and the bond holds fast.

Whatever the cause, the plan or resulting circumstances, there will be that spark of recognition that defies all explanation in earthly terms from which is born an inner trust that borders on sanctity when true friendship manifests itself. Too few are blest with such a knowledge, not many find this kind of purity, so perhaps it must be earned, or maybe it is a gift that smooths a pathway to help a willing soul help others in their turn and so pass the magic on. More likely it is an accumulation of these and many other ingredients that vary in proportion for every individual according to the need. But those who have been blest with the recognition of such a love as this, will know the value of it and know it can only be given birth when shared, and will only survive if nurtured with kindness, truth and understanding.

Yet there are other friendships, of less depth perhaps, but sincere enough according to the knowledge and needs of those concerned. They serve many good purposes in particular ways, perhaps fulfilling a need in some aspect of a person's life, whilst another friend helps balance a different part of it. But all friendships will have two things in common if they are to be worthy of the name, they all entail sharing and all are based on truth. It is from these two that many kinds of love are born that bear the name of Friendship.

Our reflections so far have wandered along the paths of human friendships, but there is another track that runs beside it, criss-crosses it and shares with it the same attributes in a slightly different form and balance. This is the friendship that evolves between human and animal lives. Man's best friend is said to be either a dog or a horse, depending perhaps on the needs of the human side of the partnership. If the need is for transport, then usually, although not always, the horse will prove to be the best animal friend, whilst a shepherd or someone who has lost their own sight, will undoubtedly find greater friendship with a dog. One fact stands out most clearly, the animal friend will exhibit a loyalty beyond compare.

We are not yet able to assess the full reasoning power of animals and so we cannot estimate their inner knowledge of us with any degree of accuracy. We do know from experience that they will trust us implicitly, rescue us in difficulty, warn us of impending dangers and even die for us if necessary. We cannot know if they are able to judge the extent of a risk in coming to our rescue, but we know that they experience fear even as we do, and must therefore overcome that fear in order to take action. It is on a par with the same situation between two human friends and must therefore share the same qualities.

Anyone who has shared a loving friendship with a pet animal, will know the ties that bind and the true unselfish affection and loyalty that their pet will give. This is the mainstay of any sincere friendship. There are some principles that apply the world over in any walk of life or death – true friendship is one of them.

FRIENDSHIP LINKS (1984)

True friendship's links are ties that bind
Not with rope or hoops of steel,
But silken threads which you will find,
Soft as gossamer they feel.

Every friendship runs its life,
Has it's purpose to fulfil,
Through happiness or tinged with strife,
True friendship grows on still.

Each friendship has it's weight and strength,
Like ships upon the sea.
Each friendship lives it's total length,
It's span is meant to be.

No true friendship can be lost,
However brief it's stay.
Some upon those seas are tossed,
Some in calmer waters lay.

True friendship always knows it's time
To greet the ebb and flow.
For God's own plan is love divine,
And always will be so.

FOR DOROTHY (1953)

Of all the gifts that are bestowed
　By God in heaven above,
The best of these from Him has flowed,
　The ability to love.
We love the earth, the sea, the sky,

Birds and flowers and trees,
We love a child, if gay or shy,
   To pray on bended knees.

We love the sunset's glorious glow,
   The moonlight's gentle hush,
We love the friends we've come to know,
   And a lover's loving touch.
But when a friend like you is found,
   Who'll never ever fail,
Our faith in God is firmly bound
   By the strongest love of all.

ANOTHER POEM FOR DOROTHY
(Slightly tongue in cheek – or cheeky)

Some think friendships grow on trees,
   Or offer it on bended knees.
Some think it just a game, and tease,
   Making friendship ill at ease.

Some people buy it in job lots,
   Or place it with 'Top Of The Pops'.
To some it is Forget-me-nots,
   Or geraniums stuck in flower pots!

But we who know the truth indeed,
   And where to plant our Friendship seed,
Know that love is friendship's creed,
   And know we can fulfil a need.

We know it comes from deep within,
   Cares not for things that might have been.
Love's future knows it's way to win
   And further friendship's kith and kin.

We know it's tears and laughter too,
   We know it's friendship pure and true
When dawn of day brings love anew,
   And friendly love it's thoughts pursue.

And so these friendly thoughts I leave,
   To grow from friendship's tiny seed
Planted when there was the need,
   To flower now, is truth indeed.

(1985)

THE POWER OF FRIENDSHIP
(December 1984)

Friendship isn't true unless it stays to help in time of trouble, for true friendship understands and gives that understanding freely, without thought of reward or reciprocation. It will stand the test of time even though those involved may be far apart in earthly communication.

Sometimes that same communication may be but brief, but in the continued life beyond the earthplane, true friendship will meet again and recognise the gentle glow, because it never faded in the first place, but remained in memory, like two parts of a whole that diverted briefly, to draw together again like magnets of the soul.

True friendship is a gift to be carefully treasured, for it is a rare and precious experience, so close to spirit communication, that at times it can scarcely be divided. Spiritual thought can span all distance and time, and thus the thoughts of true friendship likewise forge such a link that stays the course of every testing. It is perfect in itself, its perfection only altered by friends themselves, who in ignorance or carelessness can upset the balance or in purity of thought enhance perfection into holiness.

FLOWERS OF FRIENDLY CORNER
(1986)

We moved to a new house at West Coker in Somerset, where our garden was the bare earth of a builder's plot. Even the worms did not dare inhabit it at first. Friends gave us House Warming gifts of plants and cuttings from their own gardens. We put them together in one particular corner, where they grew well and blended into our own special friendly place. We have left it now for others to care for, but we did explain it's significance to the new owners, and we felt we had left them a message in flowers that would in some way perpetuate the love that came with them in the first place. It prompted the following poem, copies of which we sent to those kindly folk who warmed our new home with flowers that would stay and grow as all good friendships should.

Friendly corner is a place to stop and stare,
A place to sit, and with your heart to share
The gifts of kindly thought, still blooming there.
The roots run deep as with the roots of friendship true,
Each year the flowers blossom out anew,
And ever stronger branches greet each morning's dew.
With evening's glow, as then the sun shall set,
The warmth of friendship's hand continues yet,
For like the sun, returns unfailing, to be met
With trust and love on sunshine's heavenly beams,
Sanctified in blossoms, leaves, and honoured dreams,
These beauteous flowers come true as friendship seen,
And some, with autumn, offer fruits untold,
To prove that friendship never will grow cold,
But yet mature in strength, as we who dream grow old.

★ ★ ★ ★ ★

PROGRESSION THROUGH SERVICE

Throughout the lives of every single person upon the earthplane, there come the opportunities for progression of the soul, and these opportunities present themselves in many different ways. There are the situations where a person is given a possibility to help another who may be in some kind of distress, perhaps bodily, perhaps mentally, emotionally or even soul distress. The degree of their deed is also very variable, it may be a child or elderly person wishing to cross a busy road – as simple as that. It could equally be someone in danger of their lives, or in great sorrow because of the loss of a loved one, or perhaps be in tremendous pain or fear. Every problem for one person on the earthplane presents an opportunity to another for an expression of understanding and sympathy of one kind or another – an opportunity for action that will not only help another, but enable progression of their own soul. The only aspect of real importance to that giver, is that the thought and deed must be of spontaneous origin, with the natural desire to help for its own sake, and not from the motive of aiding their own soul's progression. That is the natural result of spontaneity, and cannot occur as a result of any selfish thought or motive.

It must always be realised, that it is only the opportunities that are given. Each must use their own sense of responsibility, their own free will, to choose whether they accept the challenge and their course of action.

In acceptance of such a situation, the giver may frequently find themselves in a position where their well meant gift of thought, action or time, may not be accepted by the intended recipient. This is of no importance. If the intent and motive are correct, the progression will take place, and a further opportunity presents itself in accepting the rebuff graciously.

Sometimes, the giver may find themselves engaged in a situation where the recipient of their kindliness, not only accepts the offered help, but wishes to retain it as a permanent prop or lifeline to their existence, and refuses to relinquish their hold, thus presenting their saviour with a further problem – how to ease the responsibility back to the original owner where it rightly belongs, whilst strengthening that person into a position where they can receive it without the good work being undone.

This is never an easy task, and as every individual case is different, no specific advice can even be given. But it must always be remembered that there are few cases indeed where all one's efforts should be concentrated on just one other person. Once a soul has become sufficiently aware, to undertake such help towards another, then he or she is on an advancing pathway of spiritual progress and is in a position to help many others, and the help they give to these others is part of their own progression. No other person has the right to try and withhold that opportunity or impede it in any way. You offer the helping hand to those in need. You try to help them into a position where they can help themselves. It is entirely up to them to know when to accept, how to accept and for how long. It is for them to learn and strengthen themselves with the help that is offered, and take the reins of life again into their own hands. The only responsibility of the helper, is to ensure that they have given sufficient time and opportunity, and that the withdrawal is gentle and in keeping with their own good motives. In this way, the opportunities are greater for both the giver and receiver.

What of the receiver? To graciously receive a gift from another, is a lesson in itself, whether the gift be of material things, or the more valuable gifts of time, help and understanding. It is never necessary to try and offer another gift in exchange. One's gratitude should be expressed to God for all gifts received, and gratitude to God is by offering one's own self to His service, by helping others in need as once you were yourself, thus passing on the true love and purpose of life, with a lesson well learned and the opportunity of one's own soul's progression – the receiver becoming the new giver.

This attitude to life then spreads the spiritual thought a little further each time it takes place, and it is not too difficult to realise the importance of such action when one visualises millions of people acting in the same manner. One million good turns can be doubled overnight, creating a brighter world not only for those living in it, but a lighter world for those in Spirit to penetrate, and give their own assistance to those in need.

It is often difficult for people of the earthplane to understand the relative differences and similarities between the individual effort and the sum total of the whole.

The individual may attach great importance to his or her thought and action, or conversely may consider the effort quite unworthy of notice, and both opinions would be incorrect. Likewise, the large events of your world may sometimes seem insignificant to the world of Spirit, whilst we yet realise and appreciate the effect that every small effort has upon the whole.

It is the whole that is of importance, and the whole is made up always of the individual thought and task, either good or bad, even as the ocean is made up of tiny drops of water, and we all know of the power of the ocean. In this simile of the ocean, it is well to remember the power that controls it, even as the power of God controls the power – great or small – of mankind.

All is a matter of balance, remembering always the strength of the individual with humility, and the weakness with determination to overcome. There are many instances in the history of man, to demonstrate the power of the individual who can influence the thinking of millions for good or ill. Their use of this power began in every single case with a small individual thought. Sometimes a small good thought gets lost along the way, often distorted by that powerful destroyer – inflated ego. Some small bad thought may also alter course upon its chosen route. A good influence upon its path may alter its destination to good effect.

The only really important aspect for the individual to remember, is the question of motive in all one thinks and does. If apparent failure seems the result at the time, it is not a matter for regret, it has its own reward which you may not be able to see at that time or perhaps from the position you are then occupying. It is sufficient to do your best to help others, and above all to take responsibility for your own thoughts and actions. By helping yourself to overcome difficulties you automatically help others. By helping others you automatically help yourself, and create the perfect balance, for by this service you add greatly to the all important whole. If you have sincerely tried your best, there is no need to burden yourself with any feeling of regret or guilt at apparent failure. If your efforts are directed toward another individual, or group of people, be it large or small, then the failure is with them, not you, any concern on your part for their opinion of yourself is irrelevant and not worthy of your attention. Probably no-one likes to be misunderstood or ill-thought of, particularly when it seems undeserved by the current circumstances. It is of no importance to the whole, but maybe of value to yourself in future thought and action, or may even be a past debt paid, of which you have not any recollection. In any case it has immediately become a past condition, of value only as guidance in the future.

If the individual can learn to keep all such matters in their true proportion, then a balance of thinking and action can be achieved, that will add greatly to individual spiritual progression and to the infinite Power of Good.

★ ★ ★ ★ ★

SO OFTEN THERE'S A FUNNY SIDE

Laughter is such an important part of life, and providing it is laughter for the right reason, can be a very healing habit. Certainly a sharing of happy laughter can help uplift others, and a truly joyous sense of humour can smooth a rocky path or help to keep a proper sense of proportion in many adverse situations. I therefore make no apologies for sharing the following poems with my readers.

The words of this first poem came pouring into my head as I stood beside a lake in Valentines Park, Ilford, one springtime some fourteen or more years ago, and I had to quickly scribble them on various pieces of paper I found in my handbag.

A young mother with a small child, was watching – or rather – intermittently feeding, the ducks. One female mallard cruised towards port, accompanied by just one half-grown duckling:–

★ ★ ★ ★ ★

TWO DUCKS IN THE PARK

Quack said the duck and cheep said the duckling,
Has anyone seen a worm?
We lost one here this morning,
It gave us quite a turn!

Two tadpoles came at lunchtime,
But their tails are very thin,
And there isn't much to live it up
On a tadpole's thin black skin.

Please have you got a minnow?
It's becoming a neurosis,
This dry old bread that people throw,
Sticks in our salpaglosis!

You've chocolate in your pocket there –
When everything else fails
Please think what it would do to us
When preening round our tails!

We hoped you'd have some grubs and things,
To ease the pangs of hunger,
But as you've really no ideas,
We'll be "dying ducks in thunder"!

What's that you say, you've got some cake?
Now you're really talking,
Quank you very much dear friends,
We're glad that you came walking.

LADYBIRDS

This poem came to me in 1984 while we were living at Wick Village
near Christchurch in Dorset. We had a lot of ladybirds at the end of the

summer, and many found their way into the house, from whence they were rescued and returned to sheltered places in the garden. This modest task of life saving prompted my sense of humour into the following verses of minor philosophy.

Have you ever wondered why
The ladybird has spots?
The brilliant armoury she wears
All spotted with black dots?

A warning sign for all to see,
That she would taste quite bitter,
That she is sour and not quite nice
As anybody's dinner!

If people too would carry flags,
To warn of sour minds,
The rest of us could turn away
When we see the signs.

Perhaps they do and we don't see
As often as we should,
The spotted human ladybird,
But if we tried – we could!

But let us not forget the good
A ladybird can do,
And human ladybirds the same,
They have their good points too!

LOVE LIVES IN MANY GUISES

I first met Jean in 1982. We arrived at her very old house towards the end of their lunchtime. Her welcome was warm and comforting after our journey. I recall a comfortable looking brown chicken sitting bright-eyed on the corner of the table, head cocked to one side, alert for any titbits that might land within her easy reach.

Before we went to the sitting room, where a lamb dashed in to greet us, wagging its tail with glee and leaving a calling card on the sofa, I noticed that a stone wall had been demolished between the kitchen and a sort of back kitchen of older times. I understood it had been in this state for quite a while, but no progress had been made at that time towards completing the alteration, and the heap of stony rubble outside the window looked well settled, as if it didn't care how long it stayed there. The thick rough stone frame that now remained, somehow made me think of a long lost monastery ruin. Perhaps it had been one – who knows? Or perhaps the dedication of long forgotten monks has something in common with Jean – perhaps the vibrations are similar. Maybe Jean's own attitude to life bears scrutiny with the simple life of monks. I have no idea, but I do know that the thought came very strongly to me as we stood there that day in a very old kitchen of uncertain pedigree.

Then all the children filed in. Some her own, some fostered – rescued from every kind of sorrow from the unfortunate to the unspeakable. The garden seemed to accommodate refugee dogs, cats, sheep and lambs, geese, chickens and goats, which I believe were supplying milk in lieu of appreciation for their accommodation. But I shall never forget the all pervading loving atmosphere that reigned supreme and bound this motley collection together, an experience of which I had never been conscious in any other home before to such a powerful extent.

Some are born into this world to give it seems, whilst others come to do the taking, sometimes because of greed or laziness, more often because of adverse circumstances beyond their own control and especially is this so in the case of children and animals. Those whose task or choice it is to give, may have no material gifts to offer but give themselves in loving service, presenting gifts of kindness, thoughtfulness and love. No questions are asked by such folk as these, no query as to whether a task can be attempted, afforded or accomplished. A blind, purposeful faith sees a need in another soul and a hand is outstretched – not to give alms or charity, but to draw that needy soul inside the circle of compassion, to share the warmth and love that only Jean types know.

The Jeans of this world are few and far between, but it has been my privilege to meet and know several, and many times I've wished I had the wherewithal to make their task the easier, but probably, deep down inside, they would not really wish it so, for the love they give to others is fed and watered by their own accomplishments. Their own achievements over all adversities, strengthens their purpose and determination to reduce the suffering they see around them in their own small corner of the world. Theirs is not to reason why, theirs is just to do or die, but guardian angels lift this breed of humanity into realms of a kind of purity. The sacrifices that they make, are the chariots that carry them through earthly life and smooth their pathway to eternity when earthly life is done. The path may not always appear so smooth to them of course,1 but as they are blissfully unaware of the many bumps and ruts they have been guided over, round, or spared in some other way, there are no regrets for such as these, just simple giving and sharing. They are the twinkling stars that seem so small, yet shed a caring light upon all darkness, and as we know, those stars are not really small, they only appear so to us who view them from a distance. I wish there were more Jeans in this world of ours, for although the rest of us may find it hard to understand them, and at times we may even despair for them, we love them for the courageous and often lonely journey that they travel in spite of the numerous lives that surround them and depend on them. Inevitably they inspire in the rest of us, a desire to help them, and so ignite in others a caring attitude, where there might otherwise be little or none – a bonus one might say, to the good already done.

We have seen her several times since then, the house is different and so are many of the circumstances, but one at least remains unchanged –

her flock of waifs and strays from every kind of sorrow – two legs or four, it matters not, they need her help and love, and Jean can only freely give it.

When we meet, something deep within both my husband Ken and his niece, strikes a mutual cord of understanding, and this link dissolves them both to tears. Some might sing, but these two cry, not in any sorrow for themselves, but something else that neither of them could explain. Is it for the suffering of humanity? Is it for the cry of animals that give their all to us and receive only harsh words and pain in recompense?

Perhaps some souls can truly feel for all the world, perhaps such love can one day save it from its own self-destruction, I think it may, for though I do not weep with tears, I share their knowledge with them and feel those tears within.

I can't begin to know the answers, but I do know that in such circumstances as these, I have glimpsed something akin to the unselfish love of God, a true compassion that asks no questions, but simply and instinctively responds.

The Jeans we meet along the way of life, not only give their love and service unstintingly, but they unwittingly prick the consciences of the rest of us. We may survey their way of life with some surprise. We may smile, despair, or some may even scorn. But we must beware, lest we judge such as these unwisely, for it is not for the rest of us to criticize the priorities of another. Their all important motive breathes life into their actions, and their actions bring help and comfort of a very special kind to others. Their pathway is a different track to that which the majority walk and climb, but their love and compassion for others, is a shining example to us all.

IT'S HARD TO BELIEVE

It's hard to believe that men once hammered nails through another man's wrists and feet to nail him to a cross. It's difficult to understand a man standing with axe in hand surveying the vulnerable neck of a fellow human being, before attacking it as if it were a log of wood. It is still harder to accept someone ordering such an action – sometimes a woman and a queen at that.

It is hard to believe that human beings would tie a woman to a stake and set fire to her, but they did. It is unacceptable to normal current thinking that men carried out severe physical torture on fellow human beings that made them scream in pain and die in agony, but it has been done throughout the ages and history of mankind and was still being done in living memory in the name of authoritative justice. In fact, such obscenities are still being practiced in some parts of the world even today.

It is shameful to those who think more clearly now, that only in the region of a hundred years past, ladies of high fashion paraded their earthly wealth and position at the expense of impoverished humanity in the sweatshops of the dressmakers art. It is sickening to accept the shoeless, hungry children in their rags while others lived in luxury, knowing of the sheer hunger and despoilment around them. In my own living memory I recall an uncle, part of whose job it was to run a "Boot and Shoe Fund" under the auspices of the local council, for children without such footwear. And all this occurring after Jesus of Nazareth had taught "love one another", and in countries where his teachings were well known and accepted.

Animals too have suffered through the years to meet the demands of fashion and fancy. The cruelties of traps and slaughter of all kinds have stained the human race with blood long after sheer necessity demanded it. The slaughter and pain continues not only in the wild, but on the farms that function specifically for that purpose.

All these things have not only happened, but are the mere tip of the iceberg – just a few facts that have been handed down to the present day, as an example of the conditions that have hidden beneath the luxury and the seas of squalor, cruelty and egoism.

In the world today, hands and voices are raised in horror at murders, bombings and self-centred people who kill and maim with careless abandon – perhaps by driving a car whilst they are under the influence of alcohol or pushing drugs to unsuspecting youth. Has nothing changed? People still demand that judicial execution should kill another in the name of justice (or revenge?), in some places of the world public executions still take place and are cheered by an unthinking crowd, and yet – there arises from the squalor of the past and present thinking, a comforting light of hope.

Through all the years of shame, there has always been the few enlightened souls that have kept alive the flame of love and compassion. Many of those who have carried this torch have been those who have themselves suffered at the hands of their tormentors, who perhaps feared them because of an inability to reach such high ideals. Yet through it all the purpose of their stand has remained to inspire others to follow and raise a voice for decency and mercy in a world of dark and treacherous thinking.

It is hard to believe that human mind and flesh can suffer so much and remain loyal to the sanctity of true love and truly gracious thinking, but it has, and the brave example of such martyrs is bearing fruit in this present age in spite of the inhuman acts that are still perpetrated in many places. Their sacrifice must never be in vain.

There is much to be done, the laurels of others must not be rested upon, but there are more and more souls recognising the evils perpetrated by some sections of the human race, both past and present. More and more eyes that recognise the beauties of the world and seek to keep them there untarnished.

It is hard to believe that beauty can rise from such cruel chaos of the mind, but when kindness can be found in many unexpected places, and efforts being increasingly made to preserve and understand the truly good things of life, a growing awareness of spiritual things and thinking, it becomes easier to believe that good can and will overcome the bad. In fact, if all the worthwhile efforts could be counted, the kindliness of so many, it's hard to believe that those efforts and sacrifices could possibly fail. In any case, we know that with spirit guidance, and with God at the helm of the ship of life, good will triumph. When you look around you and see the many wonderful kindly deeds being done in so many different places, it isn't really so hard to believe after all.

The foregoing communication was received on two different occasions, October 1989 and January 1990, and had to be amalgamated into one piece.

★ ★ ★ ★ ★

APPRECIATION

It is a strange phenomenon of the human race, that so few people really appreciate something until they have not got it.

Do we sufficiently appreciate our eyes unless our sight is dimmed or lost? Can we fully appreciate our legs and feet unless we become lame? Is it possible to truly appreciate a leaf laden tree until we stand lost in a sun drenched desert? Do we really know the value of cool clear water unless we are dying of thirst?

We can find a glimpse of true appreciation when we begin to become spiritually aware of the many gifts of God, for when the sight or sound of beauty touches the emotions towards tears, then the beauty of His creations is being recognised and acknowledged by the soul, and such appreciation can lend its light to everything that is good.

> I love to ride through tunnels of green trees,
> Where arms reach out to greet the friendly leaves,
> The murmured rustling voices sing to please,
> And golden dappled sun peeps through with ease.

I love to watch the sunrise o'er the hill,
To streak the sky with hope, and thrill
The heart with rainbow shades, and fill
The secret mind that says "Be still".

I love to know the peace that God has sent,
To clothe the secret places He has lent
For searching eyes to find His true intent
Of sacred beauty in the wonders that He meant.

I know God's love will still fulfil His plan,
In spite of all the damage wrought by man,
Yet we must try to do the best we can,
In thanks for beauty since the world began.

The foregoing poem came to me whilst riding along country lanes early one morning, having set off before the light of dawn (1989). The introduction and title came much later in 1990, as did the following soliloquy.

If you have ever stood on Yorkshire's far outreaching moors, and heard the silence blending with the larksong, or caught the plaintive cry of curlew drifting on the winds that sigh across the moorland grass, then you have touched the peace of God in pure perfection and heard the Master's voice, in the silence of the moor.

Likewise my friend, you might stand upon a rocky Cornish headland, and watch the ocean waves crash rhythmically upon the rocks below, sending foaming water leaping high in showers of salty snowflakes, without the ice to make them glitter so. Every wave is different, every pattern shines anew, awhile the lonely gull glides past you, and you hear the ghostly cry he calls to you for all the world to listen, but only you who have the ears to hear the rhythm, and the eyes to see the majesty of flight, will know that God is surely in His heaven and in the mighty splendid power of the sea.

And if in spring you chance to walk a Cornish twisty narrow lane and find her high banks glinting in the sun, you'll see the glory of her pale gold dresses – a billion primrose flowers telling you that God and nature are but one. If this knowledge comes as a surprise, then you have opened a new door to spirit understanding, but if you have recognised a knowledge that you knew before yet see it now with clearer eyes, and experience the deeper joy of recognition and pure gratitude, then you – for a brief uplifting time have been in perfect tune with God.

If it has been your good fortune to travel gently through the Exmoor countryside, then you have had the opportunity to appreciate her rounded mystic hills that dip and slide to narrow vales of lush green grass, grey rocks and wild flowers with tumbling waters bubbling gently to their unknown destination, or toppling down in small white waterfalls. The curlew flies here too, its voice blending with the skylark's cheerful song – a hymn, a strange duet in keeping with the contrasting hills and deep dark combes, the well kept farms and wild moors that feed and shelter deer and badger with impartiality. If you have sensed the peace and mystery of these, and felt the timelessness that rustles in the beech hedgerows of solid green in summer, and chestnut gold with autumn's morning dew and rising sun, then you have glimpsed the wonders of creation, the evolution of God's plan – the perfect balance that is nature, thwarting the ravages that are perpetrated in the name of progress by the foolishness of man.

And herein lies the knowledge of the power and love of God, the Great Spirit that is beyond our understanding. All such places lend their message to the ear that is tuned to listen, and the eye that sees the wonder of creation beyond the beauty it beholds.

JUNE GARDEN

June's warm evening dips her head,
  In silent worship of the day.
The brightness of the day has fled,
  And blackbird sings his final lay.

The roses bare their hearts to God,
  And offer gifts of sweet perfume.
Proud peony heads begin to nod,
  And tiny daisies close each bloom.

June's evening shadows only lent,
  To cool the heat that follows May,
Enhances honeysuckle's scent,
  And teaches all the world to pray.

But June will bring her morning blessings –
  The sparkling dew upon the grass,
Thrush will sing the early mattins,
  Heralding the day at last.

Flowers will bloom in great profusion,
  Shining with the rising sun,
Other songsters join in union,
  To greet the day for everyone.

Fledglings fuss and flutter now,
  Anxious with the passing days,
For June will teach and show them how,
  To send them on their different ways.

Then comes the dazzling of the day,
    Assorted flowers of every hue,
The buzzing bees are on their way,
    Their most important work to do.

June gardens brightly come to life,
    Stagger the mind and feed the soul,
The colours blend and cast out strife,
    To point the way mankind should go.

★ ★ ★ ★ ★

IN THE EYE OF THE BEHOLDER

Beauty is said to be in the eye of the beholder, but truth slips equally
well into this category, although we know that pure truth can have no
qualifying ingredients – it stands alone and supreme in its entirety.

There are many different religions in this world of ours and universal
agreement on two points. We all agree that there is an overall power
that in one way or another, we call God. All religions also agree that
there is life after death in some form or another.

At that point, opinions and beliefs vary and even wildly differ, but it
is also the point at which Spiritualism takes an enormous step forward.
We are the only religious organisation that has proved survival – not
once, but countless times.

It is here that we begin to see that truth, whilst supreme in its own
right, can *appear* to look different depending on the angle from which
you see it. If you look at a perfect rose from the front of the blossom, it
will appear to be different from its back view. In its perfection, it looks

different depending on the angle from which you view it. This does not alter the rose, neither does a different angle of truth alter its fundamental fact.

There are so few unassailable facts in religions as a whole, easily demonstrated by the conflicting information in the Bible. Some religious sects specialise in quoting passages from the Bible to back up their beliefs, sometimes in an attempt to condemn Spiritualism and mediumship. Anyone who knows the contents of the Bible well enough, can quote other passages that uphold both of these. We are therefore left with the realisation that we must sort the truth from the false for ourselves with our own knowledge and consciences – our own eye so to speak.

Even within Spiritualism opinions vary on some points, although many can be clarified by deeper research and understanding, and sometimes by scientific exploration. Our view of heaven or life after earthly death for example, varies with the individual. But we are told by many reliable guides and communicating loved ones, that we make our own heaven according to the way we have led our earthly lives and the progress that our souls have made, so here again we find that unassailable truth has a different appearance that depends on the way that each individual looks at it. It is in the eye of the beholder.

It is a comfort to know that however we think of God, look at life after death, or truth, they will remain the foundation of Spiritualism – a foundation that cannot be rocked or undermined, for they are pure fundamental truth. It is for us as individuals to understand the different angles from which others view this truth, and at the same time stand true to our own knowledge. We must defend truth and the rights of others to see it from a different angle – we must also preserve our own right to see it from our own, and in this imperfect world we can gather together with those of like mind, learning from each other, teaching each other, whilst accepting that others are not necessarily on the same level of understanding as ourselves. Yet we must be unafraid to follow, protect and proclaim our own pathway, that others may use us as guidelines if they so wish. Our earthly limited opinions may vary, but God and truth never alters, whichever way you look at them. It is the humble recognition of this fact that cleanses the soul and opens the spiritual mind to true progression.

In time to come, it is to be hoped that the ideal of universal love and understanding will prevail, but we have to recognise that it is as yet a long way off, and we can but play our own small part towards that ultimate perfection. Meanwhile we can only accept and deal with our present situation as it actually exists – differing views from different angles. Here it is that we can demonstrate to all, the real meaning of truth and Spiritualist beliefs, by being true to ourselves and principles by which we live, showing a tolerance to those who see it from a different viewpoint.

Truth is worth defending and preserving for it is part of the route to God, in any language, through any belief. Those who ignore truth, miss the pathway for a little while – perhaps an earthly lifetime. But in the wider concepts of true Spiritualism, we know that in the end, truth will prevail unaltered and supreme, and we shall see it in entirety when we have 'shuffled off this mortal coil' – no longer hindered by obscuring angles, no longer limited by the eye of the beholder.

Meanwhile, our own views of truth can either bind or put asunder, can bring joy or discontent, good or evil, as we choose. And we must choose aright if we are to set a good example to the world at large, and help its occupants to find a better angle from which to view God's truth and find it's beauty there.

★ ★ ★ ★ ★

OUR JOURNEY ON

Bereavement is one of our most traumatic experiences in life, and dealing with it is one of our most personal and difficult experiences. No matter what our beliefs may be about survival after earthly death, we are still left with that sense of loss of the physical presence, or a fear of our own passing.

We know that time will heal, we know we have our guides and helpers on the other side of life, sustaining us and supporting us in our time of need. We all have to deal with the difficulty in our own way, for whilst others can sympathise and help us – in the end, it's up to us.

If we ourselves are the partner that is left behind for a while, then our attitude of mind at such a time is all important, because we know if we are honest that our grief is really for ourselves. There is nothing wrong with that, so long as we realise the truth, for it is a perfectly natural and normal reaction for a little time. After that, it helps to realise that the loved one is in sorrow because we are ourselves in sorrow. If we truly love them, we must try to make them happy in their new lives. If they were only happy in life when we ourselves were happy, then that is what we have to try to do when they are beyond our physical sight, for love and emotion do not change. If we can give them the pleasure of seeing us really trying to overcome our grief, they too will find happiness that they can share with us, thereby doing the one thing they really want to do – make *us* happy. What a happy balance to experience.

This poem is a direct communication from the Spirit World to us upon the earthplane, that we may know there is no need to fear the experience we call death, either for our loved ones or ourselves – it came to me in April 1984, and has helped many people since. In sharing it now with our readers, I hope that many more will find courage and strength within these lines of knowledge.

TRANSITION

If you come to us in love and pure contentment,
And come with flights of angels to your rest,
If you come to us in peace, without resentment,
Life's journey friend, is more than truly blest.

If you've found the love and truth of daily living,
And learnt to give your soul for God and man,
Finding peace and joy in purest giving,
You add your mite to God's eternal plan.

Fear not the coming journey on towards us,
'Tis but a stepping through another door.
When time is ripe you come to join our chorus,
To greet and stay with love for evermore.

The beauty of the earth may shine with wonder,
But heavens glory dims it into shame.
Your loved ones wait for you with patient splendour,
For love where 'ere you are is just the same.

FOR A MAN OF FUN AND COURAGE

When a cousin visited us from Canada in 1988, I was eager for first hand knowledge of her father, whom I had met during his wartime service. He had visited us afterwards but I had not seen him for many years. Her father is a first cousin to my own father and the sharing of the name George Hornsey – enabled Canadian George to trace us in the first place in wartime England.

After news and memories had been exchanged, I found myself inspired to write the following poem for this much loved gentleman, now an octogenarian with so many memories of his own, including the fun and laughter when he spent his service leave in our home. His present noble age prompted the title, but it could equally be subtitled "For George, a man of fun and courage". For that is how I shall always remember him, and as my own memory rings the bells, it is good to recall someone who brightened a very dark period of our lives with his sense of fun, even while his own life seemed to be tumbling towards chaos. It is remarkable how we so often find the right people in the right place at the right time. This one had travelled across the Atlantic

Ocean to find some long lost relatives, forged a link that has remained unbroken, cheered them on their way and helped memory to ring yet another bell. Such folk are the salt of the earth and the gratitude of those with whom they come in contact will ring around the world in kindly thought and action.

FOR THE EVENING OF OUR LIVES

How blest we are to know God's love,
 That spans the world and far beyond,
His mercies shower from heaven above
 And find each soul that wanders on –
Through every joy and earthly strife,
 Collecting earthly memories,
To learn the lessons of this life
 Through all our soul's discoveries.
And through His mercies find the peace
 Which casteth out all dross and fear,
And bids the turmoils then to cease
 When only brightness can appear.

Counting blessings every day,
 Looking towards the brightest stars,
We know that we have trod God's way
 Towards His perfect joy at last,
To find adventures of the soul,
 A happiness beyond compare,
Continuous joys of life unfold,
 That inner peace without a care.
Let memories aid our journey on,
 Let love and giving be our path,
Let singing wipe out every wrong,
 And joy supreme lift every heart.

MEMORIES

The rolling hills and nature's trees,
   Gently perfumed summer breeze,
Gliding gulls from distant seas,
   Our memories enfold all these.

Shining stars on moonlit nights,
   Blending with the shoreline lights,
Silhouette the hilltop heights,
   All our memories hold such sights.

Fireside evenings, warming hearts,
   Peace descends as day departs,
While distant ships from foreign parts,
   Add memories 'ere the next day starts.

Such things can never fade or die,
   Whilst in a trice the mind can fly
To catch the echo of a sigh,
   Or flirt with laughter, lifting high.

Each passing moment of our lives,
   From fact to memory, it strives
To gild our span, and onward drives
   To God's own land, where love resides.

Sweet memories point a golden way
   Towards an ever brighter day.
And leave a dream to seek and pray,
   That other souls may find the way.

So each experience in life,
Each port of call of cheer or strife,
Adds memories beyond belief
To smooth our path to God.

These lines of poetry would become the memory of our home in North Devon if we no longer lived there. Such beauty breeds a tranquillity of mind that accepts and stores the memories for all time – the views and atmosphere etched in gold upon the gently rolling hills, and sparkle with sunlight or quiet moonlight on every flowing river or tiny tumbling stream. The peace and knowledge of silence drifts into the soul, to make and guard its memory there.

MEMORIES AND FUTURE PATHWAYS

There are three main phases to all life – the past, the present and the future. Of these, the present is the most fleeting.

Its importance lies in the fact that your present thought and action immediately becomes the past. It cannot in itself be altered or eradicated, it has occurred in a moment of the present, to become a station of the past that can only affect the future.

We scarcely realise how brief the present is, until we reflect that each word I write here is in the present, yet immediately I pass on to the next word, the previous one becomes the past, the one to follow will be in the future. Thus our whole lives are made up of these tiny moments of the present that rush towards us without pause, stay but a moment and then travel on to the past and into our memories.

We may feel we can correct or obliterate mistaken thoughts or actions, and so be careless of their nature. We cannot do this, we can only add another thought or action that will have effect upon the first to alter its result for good or ill.

If we reflect truly upon this thought, we see how important our every thought and action becomes. Nothing is ever lost, we are told by numerous Spirit guides, and as we have no reason to suppose they are not right, we must accept. Our own earthly memories may play us tricks, and alter our pictures of the past to suit ourselves, but facts remain the same whatever we may do to them.

The only true value of the past, is its effect on the present and future, which will ultimately become the present, and itself progressing into the past. To study the past is of value in assessing more progressive action in the present. To study it as an end in itself without using the knowledge gained, is a futile occupation, for all thought and action must be a progressive movement, and it is entirely for each individual to choose whether that movement is towards betterment of the mind and soul, or a worsening of the conscience towards the darker realms of consciousness. Either way the past will guide or suggest, enabling the individual to progress towards true happiness and light or slip into the darkness of despair. Freedom of the will to choose, dictates the future that will later become the present. The pattern of your circumstances is pre-ordained, the use to which you put those circumstances is for you alone to choose. The lessons of the past will help in making a good and proper choice, this alone is the value of the past.

That value lies in the memories that are collected along the route of life. Some by observation of other lives and their achievements, some by personal experience. Sometimes those memories are merely thoughts or emotions triggered by the awareness of circumstances at the time, but often our memories are centred upon people who have walked beside us for a while, perhaps but briefly, yet sometimes for a lifetime. For good or ill, their presence in our lives creates a memory from which we can always learn to fulfil a wiser, happier future.

It is our memories that bind together the past, the present and the future, the entire span of every life. They grow from small beginnings, blossom in the fullness of time according to the care we give them – the flowers of memory creating the bouquets of life.

FLOWERS OF MEMORY CORNER

Such memories the flowers bring,
Each one its message loud and clear.
Happy times that dance and sing,
Tranquil moments held so dear.

Each flower imparts its message true,
A memory shining like a star,
To guide the soul to paths anew,
Friendships linking from afar.

And even when the flowers fade,
They are not lost to memory's time,
But feed the earth from whence they came
To blossom forth in flower sublime.

And so a memory dormant lies,
Sleeping for a little while,
Yet rise in beauty to the skies,
When flowers bloom and bring a smile.

The foregoing poem was inspired by another special corner of our garden that was home to plants and shrubs that had been given to us by friends and relations. Each one had a special memory attached to it, and we were sorry to leave them behind when we moved. However, its significance was explained to the new owners who liked the idea that was enthroned in that particular part of the garden, and were pleased to undertake custody of it. The poem preserves the memories not only of that special corner, but also the pleasure that those gifts gave us and the family that inherited them.

★ ★ ★ ★ ★

"WHAT IS THIS LIFE?"

– "if full of care, we have no time to stand and stare". In this particular period of the evolution of mankind, our minds rush from one thing to another and our feet do the same thing. We are in fact so busy with so many different things, that we really have not the time to stop to see what we have accomplished, or its worth – if any. We have gained a lot and lost so much. We have learned a great deal and forgotten too much, especially have we forgotten the right way to use the knowledge we have learnt. We have jumped aboard the roundabout of progress and most of us couldn't get off if we tried, and many don't want to anyway. Whatever happened to peace of mind?

Sometimes we may think we see a glimmer of hope, for more and more people are opting out of the 'rat race' whenever the chance presents itself. They move to a quiet place in the country, feeling something akin to the call of the wild, a need for peace and quiet, while others have to content themselves with their statutory holiday in some secluded village or on a quiet seaside beach – it all begins to sound promising.

But look what happens next! The narrow streets of that secluded village are so full of cars that merely walking on the narrow pavement (if there is one) is a hazard. Heavy lorries rumble by, shaking the holiday cottage to its very foundations! The quiet beach offers other hazards besides crowds, oil or tar perhaps, broken glass and sharp tin lids washed in by the last tide, or something nasty in the sea that's bound to trigger a whole range of illnesses!

What else is there to jar the nerves of this seeker of solitude? Kiosks selling all manner of things that this seeker doesn't need, possibly there is a caravan site quite handy, or for really good measure, a bit of a fun fair, after all one must have something to keep the children quiet (both young and old). It does not seem to occur to anyone of position or authority that the fun fair is making more noise than the children (young and old!) ever could by themselves.

There *are* really quiet places of course, but no-one ever talks about them for fear they would then cease to be quiet.

But what of those who can and do elect for a quiet home in the country – possibly a second home for a year or two until retirement gives the opportunity to live there all the time – well most of it, you can't count the continued practice of holidays at any far flung place as far from home as possible, perhaps abroad or some other 'secluded seaside beach' in a different part of Britain, or maybe a flat in town for convenient visiting of friends and relations left behind, or trips to shops or places of entertainment. After all life must go on the same – mustn't it? There is nothing seriously wrong with most of these things for those who want them that way, but sometimes this chosen way of living indicates a fear of relinquishing the past rather than going forward to a new future. In this country we believe there is room in this world for all tastes and inclinations, but those who want to opt out of the metaphoric rat race and really desire true peace in quiet places, have to leave the advantages – if any – behind as well, otherwise the peace is lost. The rushing about continues although perhaps it is of a different kind and in different directions, but basically there is little change because the mind has not changed, only the circumstances.

Therefore there is no real peace of mind.

Worst of all, there are a few people who, having found their idyllic country refuge, promptly want to revolutionise it into a rural version of the conditions they said they wanted to leave behind them – and probably really thought they did. Street lighting and pavements are demanded, leisure centres and supermarkets are encouraged in this "growing area", to the dismay of the local population who tried to welcome the newcomers to begin with – after all, the village shop could do with some extra trade, now that the village has been by-passed by a brand new road, where no-one can stop and stare even if they wanted to. It is all in the doubtful name of progress, for discord rears its ugly head when the stranger wants to cut down a much loved tree, get rid of the squirrel that digs holes in the new flower beds, and exchange his cottage garden for a poor urban copy of it.

If you have wended your way through the foregoing tongue in cheek observations, you will have realised that peace of mind does not depend on any particular location. The right surroundings can help, but basically it is something that has to be fostered within the mind itself. Even the hurly burly of daily living cannot prevent a peaceful mind if the soul has learnt the art of creating and preserving it. I once knew a Col. Bartrum who had preserved his peace of mind in a wartime prison camp, by visualizing a beautiful rose in every minute detail including dew upon the petals. There are many routes to peace of mind.

First there has to be recognition of the need, a true inner desire for a tranquillity of mind that cannot be bought or acquired through material gain, and should not be confused with mere escapism. True it is, that he who seeks the rural cottage as his home to leave behind the bustle of the town, can use whatever material advantages he may have to create the conditions that he so much desires, but as we have observed, those worldly circumstances are not enough, there has to be a creative sensitivity that can use those conditions to build the peace within the mind, and that can only be done with the right inner knowledge – a sensitivity that instinctively knows the sympathetic action that blends and harmonizes. One must not only see a tree or flower, but also be truly aware of them with all their functions and achievements, in fact, love them in a special kind of way that makes them and you part of the same existence. Therein lies the key to understanding the universal love that embraces all living things and makes every part of God's creation an important contribution to the whole. An awareness of this opens the door to peace of mind.

The biting wit that digs and pokes unkindly, has no place in a mind of sensitive thinking. He who climbs to the top of his profession by trampling over others, has neither the time nor inclination for peace of mind, and she who thinks no further than an envy of a neighbour's husband or best Sunday hat, has no fertile soil in which to grow the flowers of 'Peace of Mind'. Perhaps contentment is a good beginning, the pleasure that can be found in anybody's own surroundings. That is not to say that material conditions may not be improved, but this must be in a sensitive way, with beauty in mind and a kindly thought for others, a gentle flow of thought to create a harmony that soothes the ear and eye and achieve its object without harsh discord. It is important also, to know just when to stop with creativity in material tasks, too little and you fail to accomplish your objective, too much and your project becomes garish and even ridiculous. There has to be a sensitivity to the difference between right and wrong in absolutely every field of endeavour, and that gives birth to peace of mind and begins to give the opportunity for a truly happy soul to develop it.

Once the awareness has dawned, it merely requires complete honesty of thought and kindly action to the best of one's ability. The endeavour provides the sustenance, achievement acknowledges the courage that is required, and an inner love of all living things the pathway.

When the effort has been rewarded by accomplishment, it is so much easier to take the knocks and disappointments that are part of every earthly life. Peace of mind seems to provide a shield that lessens every blow that falls and yet enhances everything of joy and beauty. Flowers seem the brighter, a lovely view can make you want to cry with an inner oneness between the scene and yourself. Some small kindly act towards you can make you feel a millionaire – as indeed you are – for you have found a state of mind that is beyond price, only your conscience can buy it for you.

This is the peace of mind that gives the time and inclination to pause and stand and stare, and what you see is the joy of pure contentment in the wonder of God's handiwork.

Peace Perfect Peace

10.10.10.10.

Peace perfect peace surround me with Thy love,

Fly to my soul you swiftly soaring dove

Lend me Thy silence, for my peace of mind,

Grant me Thy wisdom, that my heart can find.

Life perfect life, that graces Spirit's home,
Teach me the faith, to take each stepping stone,
Help me to see, the wonder of Thy power,
Grow with Thy strength, through every passing hour.

Love perfect love, that knows our every need,
Show me the way, to tend that perfect seed,
That it may grow, to glorify Thy name,
Shine on our world, to make our love the same.

★ ★ ★ ★ ★

DRAWING A LINE FOR SPIRIT

As I glance back at the spiritual route my life has taken through the years, I am amazed and humbled as I reflect on the planning ability, the guidance and patience of those in Spirit who have been an essential part of my travels, taking my hand to steady my uncertain steps.

High on my amazement and gratitude lists are the drawings I have received for this and our two previous books. They make an enticing little true story of their own.

We had sent the manuscript of our first book, *Kaleidoscope of Living Thoughts* to Regency Press, and were meeting the manager John Thorpe for the first time. We all agreed that some drawings would be a helpful added attraction, but drawing had never been one of my stronger points, and I knew I did not have the ability to produce anything suitable for printing. However, bearing in mind that I didn't know how to write books either, yet here I was presenting one for publication, I agreed to try.

In the sanctity of our Rainbow Room, our special place for meditation, healing and receiving Spirit communication, we sat together and I hopefully and uncertainly put my blue biro to paper, this time to draw. After a few tentative lines, it began to flow nicely, although I did find it a little confusing to have to draw all the lines towards me and move the paper around to create the designs!

When Regency Press telephoned to ask for the drawings urgently, I wasn't perturbed as I had plenty to choose from – until I learned they had to be in black on white. Never mind, I would simply copy the most suitable ones – at least that is what I thought!

I tried hard to copy those drawings, and Ken watched my abortive efforts and increasing concern, until at last I sat back and admitted defeat. It was at his suggestion that I sat quietly with closed eyes, listening to some particularly tranquil music, while I asked Spirit for help. It came! An explanation that àll such work had to be original, as those in Spirit couldn't copy either! I was instructed to put the old work away and put my black pen to the blank paper. This I did and the drawings immediately came in rapid succession until the required number was almost fulfilled.

Suddenly bogged down by the effort, I went for a walk and completed them on my return – almost. Somehow I could not finish the last one, but the following morning, after we had sat in meditation together, and Ken had gone to work, I picked up the unfinished drawing and quickly completed it.

When Ken returned home that evening, he discovered in the bottom right hand corner, a tiny squiggle that he thought were initials. I had assumed it was a tiny flower that fitted in with the rest of the picture. It turned out to be a monogram of the initials E.B.H. – the initials of my uncle in Spirit. On checking with some paintings of his, we found that he did indeed sign his work in that way, although I had always thought he had merely used those initials in an ordinary straight forward way.

The completed drawings were sent to press on time, and the monogrammed one can be found at the end of the book – the last drawing, a signing off – and anyone can decipher that monogram for themselves.

Later I showed the drawings to a well known medium, Betty Wakeling, who not only gave an accurate description of my uncle, but said that the artist was an engineer who worked with graph paper for designing. This was also correct, for in earthly life he had been an engineer with Fisons of fertilizer fame, and had used graph paper when designing machinery and its parts. As added proof of his survival in

Spirit, he later provided an intricate drawing of his monogram, beautifully decorated in his own inimitable style (see below).

Here then was the great happiness and proof for me of my favourite uncle's spirit presence and his discarnate ability to use my hand to draw in his own way. We had always shared a great rapport, and probably this had helped. He also provided the drawings for our second book *I'm Jane* and now they appear again in this our third. It is of further interest, that many of the drawings that were finally produced in black and white for the first book, were very similar to the original blue ones although these were out of sight at the time. Of perhaps even greater interest, is our discovery during the collation of our second book, that some of the drawings required for it had been received during the work on the first, and the same situation has been revealed for this our current effort.

On looking back in wonderment upon these things, it appears to me that a simple trust in Spirit is essential, a sincere desire to be of service for its own sake, and a humility of mind that disposes of all unworthy thought, which clears the way for such a spiritual communication. Having received it, one must use it well and honestly, purely for the purposes of Spirit. This not only assists the receiver of the communication to be accurate and maintain its flow, but must surely help those in Spirit who make so much patient effort to bring those communications to us through the dark mists around our world. When we on earth succeed, then spirit friends achieve their results also. When they are successful, then so are we – drawing a spirit line into full circle, a united effort to further the work of God.

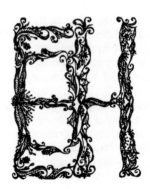

JOHN

I met John over forty years ago, and there has been a tenuous link via his brother ever since.

In 1985 I received word that John was ill with a quite serious heart condition, plus the anxiety and depressing stress conditions that so often accompany that type of illness. Spiritual healing was requested and given.

I cannot say that a miraculous cure suddenly occurred, for that would be untrue. I *can* say that there was an improvement in the physical condition, a general upliftment and reduction in the stressful aspects, that enabled him to lead a more normal life and which gave him time to adjust to the idea of eventual operation and cure, with the inner strength to cope with his situation.

At the time of the spiritual healing, I received the following poem which I felt was for John but was not sure. I asked Spirit for guidance on this point, and the next day received the drawing – his name executed in a very fine design, which only took just about ten minutes. With it I received a mental picture of his mother whom I had never met, but I knew of course that my own uncle gave the drawing, for the style was unmistakable.

This particular incident demonstrates several different spiritual aspects. The healing shows how Spirit can work with surgeons and orthodox medicine, making it easier for the conventional approach to accomplish its task.

The sequence of events over a long period of time, meant that the healing was available when the need arose and that John himself was easily able to request it, having received the necessary information and guidance from his brother who had been in constant touch with both ends of the situation, becoming the link that was needed to accomplish the fact. A fine example of Spirit planning, with everybody in the right place at the right time and with the necessary knowledge for the patient to benefit.

Friendly Spirit guides and helpers were able to provide written help in the form of a poem, a mental picture of the patient's mother, and an excellent drawing to confirm and co-ordinate the whole thing, whilst at the same time providing an interesting item for a book that was to be written years later on. The mystery and wonder of Spirit remains to elate the mind and prove its very real existence.

There is a wondrous Spirit power
For those who truly seek,
And those who seek the healing hour
Receive in peaceful sleep.

For those who trust and give their will
To use that power of Spirit,
God blesses them and bids be still,
For healing has no limit.

When precious streams of healing flow
To aid an ailing earth,
For those who truly feel and know,
Comes Spiritual rebirth.

JULY GARDEN

Perfume wafting on the breeze,
  Warm yet fresh with morning dew,
A rising prayer up to the trees,
  There for all, but known to few.

Sweet pea and mignonette are there,
  To scent the air that's angel sent,
Roses, stocks will add their share,
  Remember well, it's only lent.

Delphiniums rise in majesty,
  Reflect the sky with sundry blues,
Delight the eyes of those that see
  The heaven there within those blooms.

Poppies wave in moving air,
  Petals fine as butterflies.
Exotic blossoms fine and rare,
  And hollyhocks that reach the skies.

Early fruits come abundantly,
  To those who worked to give them life,
Rewards that come eternally,
  With July garden's pure delight.

THE PUZZLE OF SUFFERING

We've all seen it or experienced it at some time in our lives – the apparently inexplicable suffering of body or mind, or to the more discerning, sometimes the soul. Helplessly we can only ask "Why?" There appears to be no logic, and occasionally no justice either. But we know that there is no injustice in God's laws, although at times this makes our own suffering seem even more difficult to understand.

Such situations test our faith to the limits. For those without faith, the possibility of acquiring it becomes even more remote. I once received a beautiful poem from Spirit, called "Why". It was intended for a special friend, who was at that time suffering under a particularly dark cloud of circumstances. I know she will not mind sharing it now, several years later, with my readers. Being a very spirit minded person, she will hope the sharing will help others as it helped her. Curiously, all the following poems were received in the month of July, although in different years.

WHY

When clouds are scudding through the sky,
Or sadness makes you want to cry,
Each is part of a greater plan,
There always is – a reason.

If sorrow wends its way to you,
If friends forsake or don't ring true,
Both blend into a greater plan,
There always is – a reason.

Our training in this earthly life,
Is often hard and full of strife,
But God controls the greater plan,
There always is – a reason.

And when the sun shines once again,
We know we'll always need some rain,
And Nature knows the greater plan,
There always is – a reason.

When our hearts are full of song,
And nothing makes the days go wrong,
This too is part of the greater plan,
And Spirit knows the reason.

Yet for all the comfort of a beautiful poem or sympathetic friend, our hearts and minds yearn for explanation, some kind of logic that will at least make the suffering worth bearing, for so often the suffering spills over on to others – those whose task it is to stand by, watch and wait.

The simple acquisition of experience and the opportunity to learn is perhaps the most obvious reason for suffering. How can anyone know the feel of pain unless it is personally experienced, or how can anyone understand the heartache of serious disappointment or loss, unless it has been part of one's own life. Without this knowledge, how can anyone hope to sympathise and help another person in need? In order to help others adequately, it becomes therefore almost a necessity to experience suffering first hand.

Yet we meet from time to time the kindly sympathetic soul who has never themselves known serious suffering. Some nurses fall into this category, and such people can be found here and there in all walks of life. The possible explanation of this, is a previous existence, where the knowledge of suffering was acquired, and the memory of it remains with that soul, although the specific circumstances do not. Though even here, some basic instinct concerning the previous conditions may be retained but unexplained. A fear of water or sea may possibly be experienced by a person who drowned in a previous incarnation for instance – not necessarily so, but it could happen. Hypnotists experienced in the art of regression, can often uncover the source of such fears in this way.

A highly evolved spirit, whether they be part of the Spirit World or incarnating upon the earth plane will exhibit a quiet assurance and a deeply kind and understanding nature, simply because they have learned through suffering and the hard school of experience, throughout their various lives.

There are many other reasons for suffering, and it is never wise to be too pedantic in one's interpretation of any particular experience. If a soul has caused trouble or suffering to another, either in their current life or in a previous existence, then it will be a debt that must be paid – not as a punishment, but so that a lesson may be learnt and progress may be made. The debt may not be paid in exactly the same coin as the original indiscretion, but the type of experience will be the same to that person's soul. The accounts of life, must in the end – balance.

It must always be remembered that progression of the spirit is accomplished through service. No-one would have the opportunity to give this service if others were not in need of it. Thus suffering for one gives an opportunity to another, part of that perfect balance of all life and existence. It is not unknown for a soul to incarnate in such a way that they give this opportunity to someone they love and care about very much. It is the explanation for the birth of some children, who because they are not normal by comparison with others, either in mind or body, are labelled as disabled right from birth. They may even have a serious deformity with which to face life, but those whose task it is to care for them, have a supreme opportunity for their soul's progression, given to them by the selfless love of that incapacitated body of the child.

Sometimes our suffering will be because a loved one has passed to Spirit long before the time that we consider their natural span. We are left without that physical presence and find it hard indeed to face the future without that presence.

There are those who will allow such circumstances to embitter their thoughts and reasoning, thus failing to use the opportunity for progress of their own souls, and, most important, failing to help that loved one to adjust to their transition in a new life – a very sad situation indeed.

Of course that physical presence will be sadly missed, and as we repeatedly ask – Why? – Why? – Why? it is very difficult indeed to accept the need or logic of such a passing, and yet we must if we are not to waste the rest of our earthly lives, and certainly were not meant to do that. We may have to alter course, but we still have to fulfil our own earthly destiny to the best of our ability. It can help to find some purpose for our loss, a purpose that helps us to know that our loved one's life and death, and our own consequential suffering is not wasted experience.

There are so many reasons why a soul comes to earth, as many in fact as the souls that come – for every one is different, even as every person on the earth plane is different, but many will fall into certain broad categories, and any more detailed reasoning can only be worked out according to the individual circumstances. Usually it is better to accept without such close analysis – sufficient to know that there *is* some logic, that the circumstances *are* part of a plan and that there *is* someone there in control over such situations. Then we find we can continue our own earthly lives, and are able to accept the learning and fulfilment of our own destiny.

Many and varied are the reasons for coming to earth in the first place. Equally varied are the reasons for returning to Spirit apparently prematurely. What is certain, is that when a soul's mission is accomplished, that soul will return home.

So what are some of these missions of the soul, that cause them to elect for a period on the earth plane, when life could be so much easier in Spirit?

It is mostly the opportunity to learn though experience. We all know the difference between book learning and learning by experience, the nature of the former is very limited compared with knowledge gained by the latter. The soul in its wisdom knows this and chooses the harder but more rewarding path of experience. Book learning explains, experience teaches.

A soul may incarnate for a wide range of experiences, leading an entirely different earth life to anything it has known before. If the previous earth life has been rich in a material sense, the next one may be in poor circumstances, so that different lessons may be learned, and there are many other similar opposing circumstances that can provide sound reasons for a particular incarnation. But occasionally a soul may come to earth mainly for one specific purpose, all other reasons being quite subsidiary to that purpose. This can be the reason for a child's passing. The child's soul may have wanted a certain experience itself, or may have wished to give someone else, a parent perhaps, an opportunity for either progression or perhaps to balance a Karmic debt, or possibly to provide an experience that will help them in the future –

maybe to help others – the possibilities are so wide, which is why we say it may not be wise to dwell for too long on such an investigation, better use the valuable time on going forward to use the experience productively.

When a much loved soul returns to Spirit, there always is a good reason – even if we cannot readily see it for ourselves at the time.

These few examples explain only some of the many reasons for suffering on the earth plane, but serve to demonstrate the complexity of the subject and perhaps trigger the mind to further thought on the matter. There are no hard and fast rules to follow, merely guide-lines to stimulate the mind along the pathway of spiritual thinking and progression.

One fact however is made abundantly clear in all good communication from the World of Spirit. No-one is ever alone in their search.

Whoever seeks for the truth sincerely and honestly, will be guided, helped and comforted, whatever the conditions prevailing. When circumstances are happy ones, as they will be, then those same friends, helpers and guides, will share too, the joys that you find as you tread your path through life.

THE HEALING POWER OF TIME

The dreams of night,
  Forestall the dawning day.
The morning light
  Propels the birdsongs lay.
The sun of noon,
  Warming an aching heart,
Till peace of a new moon,
  Brings it sleep at last.
The tides of time reveal
  The healing power of love.
To gently make you feel
  God's power from above.

The following two poems were given by Spirit for two friends who

were at the time in great need of help for two very different reasons.
They willingly share them with our readers, confident that they will be
of help to others in distress.

FOR CHARLES
(when Betty Passed To Spirit)

God gave to us the gift of tears,
  That we might use them.
God helps us face our daily fears,
  Lest we mis-use them.
For tears and fears are part of life
  And we must live them.
Yet guardian angels soothe our strife,
  If we will let them.
And so the tears will mix with laughter,
  If we allow them.
And merge as one in God's Here-after,
  If we accept them.

Received July 1985

FOR LIZ

When sorrow tends an aching heart,
Or fear becomes the greater part
Of every passing day –
Recall the joys along the way.
Such gifts give strength in time of need,
A blossom from a past sown seed.
Picture now the perfect flower,
To comfort in the lonely hour.
Remember someone's kindly smile,
To ease the pain a little while.
For suffering never is in vain,
If from suffering we gain
An understanding of God's truth,
That joys and sorrows bring the proof

Of one Almighty guiding hand
And one supremèly logic mind.
For how could some their service give,
If every life were meant to live
Without a sadness, fear or pain?
Sometimes we grieve, that some may gain
From opportunities to serve,
And give their love without reserve.
And so the blessing is revealed
That every saddened life is healed
Which gives, receives in balanced measure
These opportunities to treasure.
The sturdy strength we each receive
In every single time of need,
Never fails if we accept
The ever loving hands outstretched,
That offer gifts of strength supreme,
The messengers of God's own dream.

Received July 1987.

STAIRWAY TO THE STARS

Throughout this book, readers will be very conscious of the fact that incidents of my early life, both large and small, have played an important part in the writing of it. This collection of memories that have rung the bells to bring messages of all kinds and purposes, demonstrate the value of our early lives to the later aspects of it. For good or ill our own early attitudes to life have a great influence on our later thinking, whilst those early circumstances themselves are of only limited influence. It is the way we have dealt with them, the lessons we have learnt from them that is of tremendous importance through all the rest of earthly life and probably beyond that.

Whatever the early circumstances, it is clear that those were the conditions that were of the greatest value to us at the time, spiritually speaking. My own early years were probably more sheltered than many and were certainly influenced by indifferent physical health, being what was then called 'a delicate child'. It is easy for me to see now the way in which these two facts have not only influenced my own later life, but also the way in which they equipped my mind to deal with the life that was ahead of me.

Probably we all have a sense of regret about certain things of the past, but as long as we do not waste our energies on blaming our circumstances, but concern ourselves with our dealing of them, then we have benefited from those conditions. When we come to this earthplane, we choose our own conditions, for a variety of reasons. Most of us are unlikely to remember making such decisions, but there is ample evidence from the Spirit World to show that this is a correct assumption. There is also evidence to suggest that the harder our life on this plane of existence, the more opportunity we have for quicker progression of the soul. It is our own soul's choosing, for in these matters we are never forced beyond our own pace, or into conditions we do not seek ourselves.

There are so many different training grounds for us to use here on the earth plane, and the physically hardest conditions do not necessarily indicate the most difficult in the spiritual sense. On the contrary, it can be quite the opposite for the simple reason that progression of the soul entails less and less of the physical, which gradually falls into less important status. We come to earth to learn, and we are told that we can learn quicker in earth conditions than those of the Spirit World. It therefore behoves us to learn well from the conditions we are given. It is for this purpose that our memories can be of help to us. On looking back we can reap the advantage of past mistakes, and early success, only the knowledge we have acquired through this life and perhaps earlier lives, enables us to truly evaluate our experiences and the way we have dealt with them, but these very thoughts that I offer now, indicate the importance of using our early years of thinking in the best possible way. If our memories are full of selfishness, crass actions, too full of our own imagined importance to the world at large, then our memories will not be happy ones, although they can still serve their purpose to teach us, providing we do not miss their points altogether. We must remember however that the best teachers in the world will fail in the task if the pupil does not wish to learn. Such children are easy to spot in earthly schooling, they do not want to learn and try to prevent others from doing so. These darker influences can sometimes impress themselves on a young person, for the young are easily influenced by psychic forces either good or bad. Nevertheless, even in early years, it becomes obvious that some children are more able to combat such influences, while others seem to welcome them. It is only the inner spiritual knowledge or the lack of it that divides children into different standards of thinking.

This hidden strata of learning has to be accomplished in conjunction with the normal social and school learning, just as later life will have to be accomplished with spiritual and earthly learning taking place at the same time. It is very important to realise that all the actions of our lives and therefore thoughts that prompt those actions, have a profound influence on the future, whether that future lies in this world, the World of Spirit or even a later earthly existence. Good thinking and action promote happy circumstances. Bad thinking and action in varying degrees promote dark and sorrowful conditions. This is not a matter of reward or punishment, it is a matter of balancing the account books of life – a case of as you sow, so shall you reap, which is not a method of learning by fear, it is a way of learning by common sense – by opportunity, by our own free will.

Many people, especially the young, feel that free will is very limited owing to the circumstances in which they find themselves. This is not so. As already described, we have ourselves chosen our own circumstances – an obvious example of free will, and we then have the choice of the way we deal with those conditions. This is the true meaning of our having free will. The balancing of our Life's Account, known to many as Karma, is for each of us to accomplish progression of the soul in the best way we can. Our early thoughts and actions can so greatly influence our later tasks in this progression, that it is often very sad for an older person to watch a younger one making too many serious mistakes. They often try to advise or guide to a different pathway, and this gives an opportunity to the younger life to benefit from another's greater experience, but still their own free will allows them to accept or discard this helping hand.

Many an unkindly small action or dark deed of woeful cruelty would never be perpetrated in the first place if these facts were more clearly understood.

Extensive experience and earthly knowledge do not in themselves indicate advanced spiritual knowledge and progression. It is not too uncommon to see a child or young person with an understanding and kindly approach to life that suggests a wisdom far beyond their earthly years. Conversely it is even more possible to see an adult of advanced earthly years failing to exhibit spiritual progression.

Without knowing their state of spiritual knowledge of the early years, it would not be possible to say whether they have advanced at all, or even perhaps taken retrograde steps in a few sad cases.

It is of great value to the young to realise their own spiritual potential. The minds of younger bodies are often more open to ideas than their older counterparts, and these ideas can be either good, bad or somewhere in between. The psychic is also inclined to be very open to outside influence in the young, and again – those influences can be of almost any strength or quality that we care to name. For the most part, our own personal Guide who is with us all through our earthly life will be able to protect us from serious wrong action and thinking, but we do have to remember our free will – that inbuilt freedom to choose our own pathway – our own route to God. Our Guides can help us choose aright – if we listen to them – or we can ignore their wisdom and loving guidance, crashing though the dark undergrowth of undeveloped ground and unknown jungle. We will not be deserted by our ever-loving Guides even when we do this, but they have perforce to stand by and merely watch until we recognise our own mistakes and ask their help to get back to wiser pathways. Our own consciences are the route back.

It can perhaps begin to become obvious that we need to keep our minds and psychic abilities in good condition, to keep ourselves fully aware of the circumstances around us. Anything which impairs that awareness puts our soul's progress at risk, and certainly inhibits the knowledge we might otherwise gain. Anything that promotes discord in our daily lives can adversely influence in this way. From drink and drugs, to disharmony, – in relationships, music, words or other acts – we can find a wrong influence that holds us back at best, or even send us along entirely wrong pathways. Once our minds are dulled to truth and kindness, we have lost some control over them, and we begin to lose control of our own lives. Only a conscious realisation of such a situation and a genuine desire to regain control for ourselves will open the door for our own Guides and Helpers to assist us. Any darker forces that have been attempting to control us or satisfy their own mean pleasures through us, will quickly recognise a lost cause, and become negative in the face of the true unselfish love of our own Spirit Guides and our own desire for upliftment.

Clearly we need not have any fear, by avoiding the abuse of our own minds, we can keep a clear pathway for our own soul's discoveries and progression. But even if we have in fact already encouraged such a downward trend, it is never too late to overcome the difficulty. All that is required is a genuine desire to do so. Most of us have an in-built knowledge of the difference between right and wrong, and if we were to follow this instinct from our earliest days, then of course nothing could go wrong to make us unhappy or spoil our outlook on life, but we have to constantly remind ourselves that we are on this earth plane by choice and to learn for our own soul's progress. This is the reason that our pathways become stony and confusing, for if we were so perfect that we need not learn more, we wouldn't be here at all. No-one is so perfect that there is nothing left to learn, either here on earth, or on the Spirit planes of life. Some may think they are, and if they do, then that will be one lesson at least that must still be learnt.

Every single person in this earthly world has much to offer towards making it a happier, better place in which to live. Too many wish to take instead of give. It is a peculiarity of life that the more you give to others without thought of reward or recompense, the more others will give to you. Learning to accept gratefully is an integral part of learning to give graciously. Age has little to do with such lessons apart from the fact that lessons learnt early stand us in good stead for longer. Younger earthly lives have a wonderful opportunity to educate their own minds and consciences towards a happier peaceful world, using the knowledge and experience of older earthly lives that have already made and overcome mistakes in life and thinking. The older have a duty to give the young this opportunity, and everyone has a duty to themselves – the time and chance to give and take in love and peace. No-one is locked out of this perpetual motion of the mind, no-one needs to hurt his own soul, for joyful life and love are everywhere for those who seek and truly wish to find them. The young in years have so much opportunity to build their stairway to the stars.

THE WHISPERING TREES

Have you heard the secrets
  The poplars love to tell?
The murmuring and chattering,
  The small talk of the dell?

The poplars know the gossip,
  They know who's who and why.
They know who makes the acorn grow
  And what made the rabbit cry.

The poplars see the secrets
  That no-one else can see,
They hear the bluebells ringing
  And sing in harmony.

Later in the summertime,
  Their leaves will stronger grow,
  Their voices will be louder
As they rustle to and fro.

If you listen carefully
  To their swishing in the wind,
The poplars tell their secrets
  To those who listen in.

WIDER THINKING

Is sufficient use made of the power of thought? Is it being used in the right way? Few people realise the many uses of this latent facility that has been given to mankind, even less is it remembered that wrong thinking can be just as potent as good thoughts. It would be to our advantage to consider these powers and make better use of them, including the wish to give this very thought impression to others, that mankind the world over may benefit from this God-given gift.

Whilst considering the subject in a general way, we should also remember the place of animals in this art of projecting thought. It would sometimes seem that they are better at it than the human thinker. Anyone who has owned a pet cat or dog, will know that they realise our thoughts and react to them long before we give actual physical signs. If for example we are going out and leaving them behind, or alternatively taking them with us, they will pick up our thoughts long before we make the signs of pending action, i.e., locking doors, changing shoes, getting out shopping baskets and so on. They will sit and stare at us, projecting the thought of their current wishes, without any other outward signs. If they need or want something that we can supply, they will sit and stare at us, silently waiting for us to get the message. It depends upon our own individual sensitivity to the animal whether or not we can interpret correctly.

Many of us feel hopelessly inadequate in such a situation, a silent admission that the animal's thought power is greater than our own. They can so easily pick up our thoughts, but we are less adept at using this wonderful gift. It is noticeable also that animals use this power amongst themselves, both in the wild and in more domesticated circumstances.

But what of our own thought power? How and when could we use it to the greater benefit of mankind? Perhaps we should first consider its uses in our own small personal world, where it is often used automatically and very much taken for granted. These personal thought-power situations serve to provide us with the proof of its existence, give us food for thought and alert us to the wider possibilities, dangers and advantages.

Most of us at some time in our lives, have fervently wished that a certain person would contact us perhaps by letter, maybe by telephone, or by personal appearance. Lo and behold – our wish is granted – "Wishing will make it so" says the title of the old song. If you consider it objectively, you have to admit that wishing is merely a strong thought process, and the stronger the wish the stronger the thought that channels it into the form of a wish.

Sometimes of course, a wish is not apparently granted, and some will use such a situation to denigrate the possibility of such a system. But there could be many reasons why a wish is not fulfilled. Perhaps the wish was not a right thought in the first place. Perhaps it is in the wrong time or place. Possibly a karmic condition will prevent its fruition. These and many more can influence the granting of a wish, but when a wish (or thought power) is strong enough and right enough, it will be so at the right time.

There are many occasions when the prospective receiver of a wish is the cause of failure. In all matters of thought transference, there has to be a sender and receiver, and if the receiver fails, then obviously the wish (thought) will remain uncollected and unused, especially if it was not strong enough in the first place to over-ride a weaker recipient, that is from a psychic point of view. Several conditions need to amalgamate together at the same time for such an exchange to take place.

Such simple considerations alert us to the possibilities of the power of thought. It could be used to much greater advantage if our efforts were more positive and better organised.

Week after week, prayers are offered in every church in the world, usually for good purpose – peace, understanding, truth etc. Prayer is but a thought directed to God – whatever our conception of God may be, according to our own religious belief. Too often, prayers offered in this way are mere words repeated with a regularity that defies the strength of a true wish or yearning.

If the object of our prayer is not capable of collecting our thoughts, then some will say that prayer has failed. Prayer does not fail, it is the human element that fails, either to project the thought, or to collect the prayerful thoughts being directed, or perhaps as already suggested, it is the wrong time or the wrong place. In such circumstances, perhaps prayers should be reformed into a thoughtful wish that the intended recipients may be alerted to the original wish that must then come after.

It would be useless to speak on the telephone until you have dialled the appropriate number, it would be equally pointless to dial just one number and hope that a dozen or more would hear the call, the first receiver would have to be asked to pass the message on. So why should anyone expect a blanket thought – for peace for example – to be collected and be fruitful if we have directed it to no one in particular? God will hear, but God needs the goodwill and co-operation of His earthly students in order to teach life's lessons and fulfil his plans.

There must be countless numbers of thoughts drifting around with nowhere to go, depending on casual sensitives to be aware of them. This can easily happen. Many sensitive people will be conscious of having a sudden thought come into their heads, with no knowledge of its origin. They will probably not even pause to ponder on the matter, merely acting upon the thought if it seems a good one or dismissing it if it seems to have no relevance for them. Pause here for a moment to wonder where ideas come from in the first place – the brain perhaps – but who starts them off in the brain? The question is especially pertinent when those ideas have no apparent connection with the owner of the brain or anything that particular brain is dealing with at the time the thought entered. Most people agree with this principle when they affirm "An idea came into my head the other day . . ." – almost without realising what they are saying.

We can now come to the consideration of wrong thinking – wishing for something that may be selfish or even morally wrong. These thoughts have the same power as good thoughts, and as we humans often have stronger feelings of dislike, annoyance or hate towards others than the opposite conditions, we are clearly able to do much harm with even our casual thinking. If we deliberately project hateful and bitter thoughts towards another person, we may do very much more harm without consciously trying, than we can do good with our kindly projections of thoughts that require a strong conscious effort on our own part. It is easier to dislike or even hate than it is to truly love when hearts and minds are out of tune with each other.

The power of thought has been known and used throughout the ages of mankind, for good and bad effect. The art is still practised in some primitive societies, and here and there in advanced ones, but has been largely lost in more material and technical environments, but it can be resurrected at any time we choose, and its use could be a great influence upon our world for either good or ill.

Those upon the earthplane with true concern for others, and a true longing for the cessation of cruelties, selfishness and greed, could band together in powerful thought towards this end. The power of wrong thinkers should be borne in mind, those who wish to inflict upon the world their egotistical lust for power, the power that delights in the suffering of others, the dark satisfaction that wallows in the selfishness of misdirected power. These wishes are so strong in some people that their 'thought power' can make it so.

Those of good intent need to gather their forces and strength together, channel the power of good thoughts towards the greater good for all. This is a way to combat much of the evil thinking that exists in the world.

It is a frightening thought that those of ill intent could use this thought power to influence others on a world wide scale, and many in their ignorance would be helpless against the onslaught. Investigations are being carried out in this direction in some parts of the earth, and it is entirely up to those with an awareness of thought power to make sure that the thoughts for good outweigh the evils of wrong thinking. It is time for all to make a more concentrated effort towards good and kindly thinking, in a strong and positive way that will benefit all mankind, and spare all living things from the horrendous results of projected wrong thinking. Positive steps could be taken now towards this end, using the gifts of thought power for good purpose, that everyone of right thinking may play a part towards happiness and peace throughout the world of current sorrows.

The power of thought can be used in so many ways – healing the sick and suffering for example. It is such a useful ally towards the upliftment of someone who is burdened with cares and worries. Thought can sometimes be a very direct way of contacting someone in need, by-passing the more conventional and time consuming methods. Anyone in distress, wherever they may be and at any distance, can be helped by the power of thought.

Yet it should never be forgotten that the power of thought can also be used for ill purpose, and *that* power must not be underestimated, for earthly history has shown that whole nations can become involved with evil as a direct result of wrong thinking in their leaders, possibly even those leaders have been influenced wrongly by just one person.

It is entirely up to the individual how he or she uses this gift from God. It must be remembered also that the powers of good thinking are the work of God, who will strengthen the efforts that must ultimately overcome evil, because God is the all powerful force. Those who are His instruments of peace and love must use their own strength and knowledge, for it is then that the power of God uses and consolidates those efforts, and lends the greater strength.

It would be a wonderful thing, if at a certain time each day, perhaps noon, a moment was spared to project the power of wider right thinking towards someone or some situation in the world, with the purpose of clearing bad or negative thoughts from that quarter. Imagine the enormous power released at that moment of daily time, and as noontime falls at a slightly different time around the world, this healing power would be a continuous stream of thought towards an international peace.

United thought at a given time is not an essential, as good and kindly thoughts are never lost. Nevertheless, it has been shown that the human mind of one person can stimulate the thoughts of others without a word being spoken. It follows that a united effort at one time can generate a greater power at that time, each thought from each thinker stimulating others towards good. A wonderful and wider power for peace and happiness cast upon a very needy world – a noontime world-wide thinking for healing.

AUGUST GARDEN

The brilliant warmth of an August day,
Nostalgic scent of new mown hay,
A mass of flowers in fine array,
To teach us mortals how to pray,
And bless an August morning.

The blaze of August's annual flowers
Fed by swift retreating showers,
Blest by sunshine's warming hours,
Dazzled by the floral bowers
To bless an August noontime.

A pansy shyly lifts her face
In modesty, she knows her place,
Covers the soil with charm and grace,
Enchanting any vacant space,
In the August afternoon.

The breathless hush of summertime,
Murmuring voices soothe and balm
The air, that hovers sweet and calm,
Over garden, field and cairn,
To bless the August evening.

The skylark's evensong has ceased,
And sultry night has now increased
Nocturnal flights of quiet peace,
And petals close, their prayer released
To bless an August night time.

Yet now the blackbird sharply calls,
A rising morning song enthralls
A listening ear – which then recalls
The power that nature's plan installs,
As a sunblest August dawning.

And so Man's ills receive some pardon,
Through the joy of August stardom,
As colours scramble in profusion
In every corner, quite unbidden,
To bless each August garden.

REFLECTIONS

The words that inspired the following thoughts, are on a poster of a beautiful sunrise. The picture caught our attention in a shop in Boscombe, and we hung it on the wall of our Rainbow Room, where we sat in quiet meditation, or concentrating on healing thoughts for others. It is the place where the communications for our first book, *Kaleidoscope Of Living Thoughts* were brought to us through trance mediumship. The poster was opposite my chair and was always an inspiration, first for a hymn, and then in August 1982, these thought provoking reflections:-

"Shine on me Father, that I may reflect your light" – a prayer so beautiful in its simplicity. Not a request for help with some worldly problem, just an offer to serve, prompted by a serene and hopeful sunrise.

We can find reflections in so many things apart from the obvious mirror. A still lake or river will reflect the trees or buildings on its banks so well, that if you photograph the scene you can look at the print either way up. Only close inspection will reveal that the reflection is not quite the same as the original.

Sunrise or sunset, or a full moon reflected across the moving sea making a pathway of light, breathtaking in its beauty and serenity, and acquiring a strange mysticism all its own, lent perhaps by God, to stay a little while, then leave us to reflect upon its wonders.

Less obvious perhaps are the reflections of happiness on the faces of people. A mother's loving smile for her baby, will produce a happy reflection on the baby's face. A loving glance from one person to another, will be reflected on the face of the recipient. A kindly act too will shine out from the giver to the receiver and be reflected there, and the pleasure of the receiver reflects back to the giver.

The real wonder of these reflections, is that they may not be for just the two people directly involved. Anyone who is near enough can witness this shared joy, and thereby accept a small portion for themselves. In their turn, they can be so uplifted that they will unconsciously pass on some of that reflected light to even more people.

The light of God, the beauty of Spirit is a wonderful thing to pray for – selfless by nature, setting in motion a crystal of happy, uplifting thoughts and emotions to sparkle and shine as they flash from one to the other.

But we must not forget, all that beautiful light will be lost if it falls on a dark rough surface. Our Father can give us the spiritual light, but we are the waters and mirrors that can reflect it. We should try to keep ourselves calm and smooth as the still waters, or polished as a clean mirror, so that we may reflect that light and love and send it rippling away and beyond, that others may share it. "Shine on me Father, that I may reflect your light" – and please lend me a duster to polish myself up in readiness!

Shine On Me Father   (L.M.)

Shine on me Father that I may, Reflect your light in every way,

Help me to see through darkest gloom, the light of love the brightest moon.

2. Breathe on me Father, that I may
   Feel the warm air of glorious day.
   Help me to know, and never fear,
   Thy glorious presence, ever near.

3. Speak to me Father, that I may
   Hear your dear voice, through every day.
   Help me to hear and understand,
   My Father's voice, His healing hand.

4. Smile on me Father, that I may
   Reflect your love in all I say.
   Help me to be, a soul of love,
   Sharing Thy light, from spirits above.

(This hymn may also be sung to the music of
      Lord of all being, throned afar)

THE CASE FOR ANIMAL SURVIVAL

Throughout the ages and evolution of mankind, animals have played an important part in his life. Ever since primitive man learnt to trap and then hunt animals for food and clothing, animals have been of increasing importance in the development of the human race.

They have, in addition to the provision of food and clothing, displayed an aptitude for service that would put many human beings to shame. They have for instance, turned wheels to pump water or grind grain. They have carried people on their backs through appalling conditions of terrain and war. They have borne over heavy loads of goods and chattels and pulled carriages and tramcars full of people. They have rescued from mountains, rivers and collapsed buildings. They have fertilized soil so that vegetable crops and grain can be grown. They have carried life saving messages when no other type of communication was available. They have given pleasure and excitement to billions in the way of sport and pastimes. They have suffered and died on behalf of people, the mental and physical pain of experiment, and inspired great works of art. They have enabled some to experience great depths of emotion, inspired others towards fine achievements and the glory of God. They have comforted the lonely, taught us the true meaning of loyalty, service, and above all, the sanctity of unselfishness.

Yet through all this and the thousands of years it has taken for these things to occur, many people still regard animals as subservient beings, or as useful but unfeeling avenues for their own purposes of gain or greed, and targets for their own inadequacies and power, as expressed in bad temper, cruel instincts and lust for mastery over others, to name but a few.

Through all this, animals continue to serve mankind unselfishly, which leads some people to consider them inferior and worthy only of scorn and contempt, much as human servants and slaves were disrespected in dark past ages by many in high places.

Mankind in his thoughtlessness or ignorance, overlooks the fact that everyone who incarnates upon the earthplane has come for a specific purpose, and his or her place in society is governed by that fact. They also overlook the fact that animals also have a part to play in those purposes and a position of their own to fulfil, which does not mean being on the receiving end of man's cruel streak.

Certain animals have evolved along with their human counterparts because mankind was able to make use of a natural tendency in some animals to associate with the human race. It is debatable whether mankind himself brought this about, or whether the animals were themselves ready for this step forward. It is worth noting that while some animals have shown themselves to be readily adaptable to human ways, they are in the minority. The great majority remain in varying stages of wildness, and most show no tendency to consort with the human race. When it does occur, it becomes more far reaching than greater development of the brain. There is considerable and often indisputable evidence of survival of the spirit of animals, thereby proving beyond doubt the existence of spirit amongst the animal kingdom. Whereas some animals with a physically large brain – dolphins for example – have not given much evidence, although exhibiting an attunement with man in earthly conditions, others have given very positive evidence, particularly pet animals that have had a close and love-exchanging relationship with their owners. Even birds have succeeded in making their presence felt – sometimes seen or heard.

The nature of animal spirit, is as yet no clearer than that of the human. But as the human being is also part of the animal world, it is likely that their spiritual make-up is at least similar, for as with the human being, it does appear that affection provides a link that makes it easier for a spirit to contact an incarnate soul. It is known that spirit in some form is with all life, people of long, long ago were aware of the spirit of trees for example, and even today when much of this instinctive awareness has been lost in the human race, many are conscious of the healing strength that can be obtained by leaning against a well matured tree. Many others automatically and unconsciously like to walk among trees because they feel uplifted or better in some way or other by doing so.

It is possible to photograph the emanation that surrounds all living things – that which we call the aura, and it is now realised that this can be seen around anything which has life. When life has ceased, so does the aura become invisible to the human eye and camera lens. Scientists may well find eventually, all the constituents that combine to produce this phenomenon. Amongst them will be that part which is associated with Spirit – that ethereal something which we know is there and yet evades our knowledge. It is of interest but not really important to know the ingredients since we have the whole in all its wonder.

The fact that every living thing is equipped in this way, adds much authenticity to the reports we are privileged to receive from time to time from the World of Spirit about the beauty of trees, plants and flowers on that side of life. Dare we hope that all this type of beauty we can see here upon the earthplane, does not after all die and rot away, never to be seen again? Dare we visualise that the spirit of flowers and trees can collate into even greater beauty, and grace the World of Spirit to an even more glorious degree? Why not? This very fact has been communicated to us upon the earthplane many times through the years. It is only our own lack of comprehension that limits the view. If this is the future for trees and flowers, and we know that we ourselves survive earthly death, then of course animals must do the same, it could not be otherwise. The nearer to the human race those animals have been on earth, the more developed the spirit can be.

Amongst the domesticated animals it is quite easy to recognise similar traits of development to that which we see in ourselves and our fellow human beings. Some good, some bad and a whole gamut of different standards in between. Some dogs for instance display a kindly type of nature, whilst others can be quite the opposite – just like their human counterparts, and it cannot necessarily be explained in either case by the upbringing of the individual, for both good and unsatisfactory early life can bring about good, bad or average adulthood in either human or canine form. The basic nature of the individual either rises above difficulty or succumbs to it, which itself suggests a higher spiritual development in some than others to start with.

The majority of domestic cats seem nearer to their original wild state than most dogs and are therefore usually less developed spiritually, and less likely to be of a kindly disposition. Some however are. Most of us have at some time in our lives known of a cat that will 'mother' a mouse, or play gently with it. Such a cat will gently pat a butterfly without harm to it, smell flowers in the garden or show a friendly tolerance to the family dog, even displaying affectionate trust towards it where in the wild they would be enemies or take care to keep at a safe distance.

Looked at in this way, it becomes clear that our pets are not only endowed with Spirit and survive death, but will be at varying states of development just as we are ourselves. When we consider the way in which some human beings behave towards both animals and their fellow man, we may perhaps be forgiven for thinking that some animals show the greater progress, indeed in certain cases they probably do. But that is another matter. Here we are looking at the case for survival of the spirit of animals, and logical consideration of the known facts tells us it must be so.

But we are frail in trusting our own logic and slow to embrace the truth when we see it, for fear of looking foolish or being wrong – and so we seek for more proof. In fact, we usually only accept a situation as proof when it happens to ourselves. Second-hand proof is rarely enough, but it does have its uses. Someone else's proof of survival of either human or animal survival can open the door for us, alert us to the kind of evidence that – if we think about it – can become our own proof that our loved ones are alive and well after earthly death. Truly we can be shown that our much loved pets do survive and are cared for by people they know who love them too. We can be acquainted with the fact that they are often around us still, and share with us some of the daily incidents of our lives. Those little things that help our human loved ones to make their presence felt after their passing to Spirit can also give our pets the opportunity to do the same. It would be sad indeed to deny them the pleasure of recognition. We know how delighted they are to greet us when we return home after an outing they could not share – would we then ignore their enthusiastic greeting? Of course not – we accept the loving joyfulness they offer and give our own to them in return. Obviously it would be most unkind to sadden them by ignoring their presence when they return to us from the World of Spirit. No need to be ashamed of having been aware of your pet's return, it certainly would not do so if it did not wish to. So when your pet does come to you, don't ignore it, use the knowledge you have gained to recognise it and bring happiness to you both. In doing so, you will have acquired an experience that you can pass on to others, so that they too may become aware of the Spirit survival of their own pets.

To illustrate my point and give you the opportunity of benefiting from my own experiences, I will tell of some of the occasions when memory rings the bell for me, and I knew the pleasure of my pet's company again and the comfort that such a return can bring.

Some years ago I visited London Medium Jessie Nason. Amongst some very accurate information concerning family and friends in Spirit, and thereby proving their survival, she mentioned animals with which I had been connected or owned, including three Alsatians and a Yorkshire terrier. She explained that one of the Alsatians often made its presence felt by bumping me in the back of my right knee with her backside as she humorously described it.

This was an extraordinary piece of survival evidence, for in earthly life, my Alsatian Judy had a curious habit of swinging her tail end round to knock behind the right knee as she passed by. This was a dog with a great sense of canine humour, who played this little game with glee, judging by her saucy glances back at me, the gaily waving tail and mischievous gambol that followed, and I had often experienced it *after* her passing.

In my ignorance at the time, I had assumed that my own mind was conjuring up a happy but nostalgic memory, but Jessie had opened my mind with the aid of a dog. She told me to always acknowledge the greeting, which would encourage the dog to continue with it and help to maintain the link. I have done so ever since.

Whilst living at Wick Village, our dog at the time was another Yorkie, Tina. It was while we were there that both Ken and I became conscious of the presence of another of the same breed, that we often nearly fell over it as it suddenly moved so near our feet. We assumed it to be Tina, only to find her alive and well somewhere else on the premises! This turned out to be Penny, Tina's predecessor, who did in fact have a habit of sometimes getting under people's feet, something which Tina never did. So acknowledgment was again called for! In our present bungalow, we have both seen briefly, a small almost black animal on a number of occasions and at first have thought it to be our own Poppette, again only to find her asleep elsewhere! Unfortunately we have not yet been able to identify this one, but we acknowledge the appearance just the same, and hope one day that we will find out who this little one is.

I could add many more experiences about animal survival, but will content myself with one more – about a cat. Also whilst at Wick Village, we used to visit Ken's cottage in the New Forest every Saturday morning to cut lawns and tidy up in general. One Saturday, after Ken had left the car and walked up the path and into the house, I followed within a few minutes. By the time I reached the door he had returned to the car, leaving the front door closed but not fastened. I pushed open the door and stepped inside, and as I did so a black and white cat rushed past me into the garden. I assumed it had gone into the house when Ken arrived, and I turned to look and see where it had gone, but it was nowhere in sight. After pondering on it for a short while I asked if he and his first wife Myrtle had ever owned such a cat. They had! In earthly life cats are frequently known to associate themselves more with places than people, and when moved away from the favourite haunt will sometimes negotiate considerable distances in order to return to it. Clearly this particular cat would have no reason to make its presence felt to me personally, but every reason to let someone know that it visited its own old home, and it was my privilege to be the witness.

I hope these incidents and observations will help someone somewhere who has grieved because a much loved pet has died. If my bell ringing memory has done so, then I am happy to have been of service.

★ ★ ★ ★ ★

I REMEMBER WHEN

I remember when my dearly loved Grandfather gave me my very first garden. I was about five years old and the patch of garden – on looking back – must have been about 6ft x 4ft. Escallop shells provided the demarcation line between my own and everybody else's garden, and the soil was well dug to start me off on the right gardening foot. I can see it now in my mind's eye, near a rustic arch that was covered with American Pillar roses all summer.

Grandad gave me four packets of seeds, two of flowers and one each of lettuce and radish. I also had a small rake, hoe, trowel and handfork in keeping with the size of my hands, and plenty of guidance in the use of them.

This fostered in me a love of flowers and gardening that has stayed with me ever since. It sparked an interest in growing vegetables for our own consumption, and I well recall the pride of achievement I felt as I cut my first lettuce to offer to my mother. My gardening taught me a love of nature and the gentle patience that is required for all aspects of this noble art. It introduced me to the functions of birds and bees, giving me a sound and simple grounding of the knowledge of life at an early age. I shall always be grateful to my mother's father for this gentle but positive beginning.

I remember that little garden too for another reason entirely. At a local fair I had won a goldfish in a bowl, by rolling pennies down a wooden chute on to marked squares on a board as I stood on tiptoes peering over the edge of the brightly lit round stall. None of us knew then that goldfish should not be kept either alone or in a small round prison bowl, so this one died after a few weeks. It was my first experience of death and I remember my confusion and lots of tears. I expect the whole family tried to comfort me, but it is Grandad that I remember clearly, taking me to my tiny garden and helping me to bury the goldfish in a small wooden box my father had made. As we laid those small remains to rest, Grandad explained about going to heaven and being cared for there. A small cross and a special plant in flower marked the spot in the left hand corner at the back of my little plot. Whether he actually believed himself that my fish would survive death, or whether it was a kindly explanation for a very small, unhappy girl I may never know. I do know that my tiny first garden taught me many things through the wisdom of my Grandfather. I wish that all children were as fortunate as I, to learn the truths of life through gardens, nature and a very wise and kindly Grandad.

I remember when I was on holiday in Yorkshire with two friends. They were soaking up the August sunshine on a quiet beach, but this particular luxury never really suited me, so for a little while I followed my own inclination, with sea on one side and ripe barley on the other.

I walked alone along the clifftop and no one else had chosen that footpath at that particular time. Perhaps I was meant to feel the wonder and the peace all by myself, perhaps I could not have become so aware if any other person had been present. But now, some twenty years later,

I have come across the poem that flooded into my mind as I walked that morning. The lines were hastily scribbled on an old envelope, that ever useful receiver of the unexpected message and preserver of thought when memory alone may fail. Perhaps now is the time to share those precious moments, that others may glimpse the serenity that I felt then.

A WALK ON A YORKSHIRE CLIFFTOP

There's singing in the cornfield,
There's singing from the sea,
Nature's choirs of music
Are singing just for me.

A lonely Yorkshire clifftop,
The breeze sighs through the grain,
The rhythm of the pounding waves
And the rushing back again.

The sounds are music for the few,
For those who tune to hear,
For nature's songs are secret songs
For the truly listening ear.

There must be something special about Yorkshire, for two years earlier in another part of the county, I had shared a holiday there with my parents and captured some of the magic in my memory and on yet another old envelope. I had stood on an old stone bridge that crossed the Swale, watching the waters bubbling beneath – a fish darting here – a willow dipping there – and a duck – drifting with the flow of the river, demonstrating a true economy of effort for its own purpose – whatever that purpose may have been.

The silence, but for the water, had to be heard to be believed. It was the first time that I remember being conscious of hearing silence. They were moments to share – much later, via the following two poems that came to me at the time.

A QUIET THOUGHT OF YORKSHIRE

If all the world could feast its eyes
   On Yorkshire's rolling dales,
If all the world could synchronise
   With Yorkshire's lovely Swale,
If all the hideous things of life
   Could find confession there,
If worldly sorrow, fear and strife
   Could find it's soul to bare
In Yorkshire's tumbling waters cool,
   And mystic wolds and ancient trees,
And find God's truth in crystal pools,
   Then all the world would find it's peace.

THE MYSTERY OF THE SWALE

There is a mystery that I know,
   In a rippling Yorkshire stream,
It has a tumbling, tinkling flow,
   That mirrors a sparkling dream.

It winds and dips beneath the trees,
   It's rushes reaching high,
It bears along the floating leaves,
   The willows swish and sigh.

You follow it for mile on mile,
   How big the fishes grow,
Sometimes still water rests awhile –
   But where ever does it go ?

Having spent yet another delightful holiday with our good friends
Dorothy and Ron Middleton in a pleasant converted granary not far
from Yorkshire's Pickering, we visited Hutton-le-Hole, which inspired

the following poem. Perhaps I was helped by the kindly Spirit entity that made his presence felt in our cottage near the moors. It was a wet and windy spring in 1985, when sunshine bravely battled with the elements, determined to prove superiority, when a knowing horse guessed the times when we would set out on our daily jaunts, and begged a biscuit over the field gate. Tina, our 15 year old Yorkshire terrier ran and danced like a two year old and paddled happily in clear shallow streams with the joy of invigorating moorland air. We giggled our way through low clouds as if we were flying, and chuckled our way through a driving snow blizzard that dared to poke it's nose among the daffodils and made the moorland white in a few seconds, for after all, it was cosy enough in the car with good company for good measure. We joked as we prepared our meal in the comfortable kitchen of our cottage, and sat cosily round the fire in the evening re-savouring the day's events, and the Spirit gentleman revealed that he had once kept the granary swept clean. Perhaps he still did because it never seemed to get dirty. Perhaps all these things combined together to produce these verses.

THE PEACE OF THE YORKSHIRE MOORS

The quiet peace of Yorkshire's home,
Rippling streams and solid stone,
Soothes the soul and warms the heart,
Helps the mind its love impart.
It lends the strength to forward stride,
To live a life with humble pride,
When elements bridge timeless days,
And guide the soul through safer ways.
While smiles and mystery pledge their troth,
To blend all minds and souls – or both
Into a harmony of peace,
That discord may for ever cease.

DOWN ON THE FARM

I remember when great chunks of my life were spent on my uncle's farm. So many of my early memories are associated with Stonebridge Farm in North Somerset, that they compete with one another for recognition and would fill a book themselves – given half a chance.

My earliest memories are associated with chickens, as I held a bowl of corn and was allowed to toss the contents out twice daily. I would be about two or three years old when I enjoyed this privilege (for privilege it certainly was) and I particularly recall a large pushy 'father bird' that scared me just a little bit, so I threw more in his direction to keep him occupied at a safe distance. This was probably my first lesson in dealing with unpleasant people who were stronger than I. They seem to succeed while others bow to their greater strength, but the more they get, the more they want and return ever quicker for whatever spoils are in the offing – certainly that cockerel did! – until my uncle told me to stamp my foot at him and throw the corn in the opposite direction. This had the effect of making him run further for his corn and kept him better occupied – a satisfactory way of dealing with his human counterpart.

Letting my mind wander amongst chickens of the past, makes me pause to consider how sad it is that so few of them now enjoy the happy freedom of those birds so long ago, and it cannot surely give the same feeling of delight to collect eggs from a trough in front of a row of cages, as I felt in hunting out the nests in strange places and the sense of pleasure in finding them. Some will say we should not eat eggs or keep poultry anyway but that is another matter which is not included in my current mental trips into the past.

As memory rings the bells again, I recall Punch, the heavy farm horse which I was sometimes allowed to ride in later childhood, although I can remember sitting on her back at a very early age. Punch was broad, quiet and safe. She was so wide that I experienced some difficulty in getting my legs down her side to give the required signals with my heels gently on her flanks. What a noble creature is a horse, I learnt it then and know it still, for how this gentle giant used her strength contrasted sharply with the cocky cockerel of my earlier experience, and is perhaps a lesson to us all on the use of any power or strength we may be given. We may use it kindly and with discretion to help others and thereby ourselves, or we can seek to dominate and force our ideas and power on others entirely for our own purposes. The horse seems to know better than we do in such matters in some cases.

I helped to make hay on the farm and fed the calves, putting my hand in the bucket of milk, letting these babies suck my fingers, drawing up the milk at the same time. Here was an early lesson in caring for the young, along with the fluffy yellow balls on legs that seemed to roll in sudden dashes around the farmyard with their mother hen, and the lightweight little bundles that bobbed on the stream with the mother duck – all so vulnerable, all in need of kindly attention and concern. I don't recall associating those lovely velvet-eyed calves with the veal that I sometimes ate, I suppose I was too young to know such things. But in later life, the memory of those babies put me off the eating of it, probably my earliest leaning towards vegetarianism, which came later, but undoubtedly those calves were an early start in that direction and served to demonstrate how early experiences can influence our later lives.

Hay-making was fun as well as work. We tossed it with peaks (two pronged pitchforks on long handles) to let the air and sunshine do it's work as well. We piled it into cocks, and as the hay wagons came round, drawn by our faithful Punch and another horse lent for the occasion by a neighbour, we piled the loose hay up high, while someone on the top spread it around evenly to prevent a hay-slide as the wagon jogged its way across the bumpy field – an art that is probably almost lost now that hay and straw is normally baled in the field.

My mother's younger brother – my favourite uncle, used to bring some members of his motor cycle club to stay for a week on the farm, and this added much excitement to the normal farm routine. As I recall, they were high spirited but disciplined young men, along with some wives and girl friends. Hay fields were cleared in no time at all with their enthusiastic help. Food appeared and disappeared like magic amongst the grassy stubble, and the chickens took a dim view of motor cycles in the yard and made squawking dashes for cover. The girls made apple pie beds for the men, sewed up pyjama legs and put teazels under their sheets, or rather they got me to do that part for them, so that they could innocently and truthfully say that they hadn't put those prickly objects there. No one ever suspected me of doing such a thing, though they could rightly have pointed a finger at my mother, who was usually up to every trick of innocent fun you could think of. Pillow fights often ensued, and wash-basin jugs of water were handy for preventing the opposition from mounting the stairs. We laughed until we nearly cried, a good time was had by all and any damage was duly paid for, and any mess – like the contents of a burst pillow – cleared away without trace. I sometimes think my own sense of humour was nurtured there amongst the hay, the pillow fights and teazels.

My farming uncle and aunt were such excellent examples of tolerance, and in their turn gleaned the upliftment that these unusual visitors had brought to the staid farming fraternity for just a little while. Not that my aunt was lacking in humour, on the contrary, she was in the fun with the best of them, aiding and abetting in every way she could. My memory tells me that Aunt Liza and my mother made a very effective comedy team. I clearly remember them dressed in an assortment of male attire walking up through the village and back giving a fair imitation of Charlie Chaplin, amidst much mirth and frivolity. It was quite a daring thing to do at the time and I dare say brought a few disapproving frowns as well as the laughter. What a priceless gift it is, to bring about spontaneous laughter without fear or harm to anyone or any thing. Too few possess it, too few acknowledge it.

The visitors themselves opened unsuspected doors to us all, with their kindness, their willingness to learn the mysteries of the countryside and their appreciation of it. We played football, flew kites and sang round the sitting room piano. Such memories serve to demonstrate the value of co-operation, of tolerance and understanding of another's way of life, and above all perhaps, a sense of kindly fun with personal responsibility towards others. They serve to show us how words and deeds in our daily lives amongst the unimportant things, can set a pattern of thinking – not only for ourselves – but for all with whom we come in contact – for good or ill. I was fortunate that so many of my early memories brought laughter and were based on life at that particular farm with all those special people.

A POPPY FOR BETTY

I remember when I walked with two friends and their two small children in a very old and narrow Essex country lane. Nearby behind the hedge, the wider, newer road took the traffic on its way, leaving our secluded spot to return to nature with its profusion of tall grasses and wild flowers. Honeysuckle wafted perfume to the air, and wild roses bravely claimed their right to be there, both attracting bees to add a soft humming as a kind of background music to the peaceful country surroundings.

We were collecting clues for a car treasure hunt that we were organising for our theatre club. This place looked promising for clues and a pause in our endeavours.

Along the way, I had remarked several times on the lovely splashes of red poppies at the roadside. I'm not sure why these flowers appeal to me so much, perhaps it is the silky delicacy of their petals, maybe it is the brave resistance of such frail flowers to all winds and weather, or their bright colour may have an uplifting effect, or perhaps some hidden knowledge of a far away battlefield that my father experienced. I know not why, but appeal to me they do.

Suddenly, young Jane emerged from grasses taller than her three to four years permitted her to be, carrying the largest wild poppy I have ever seen. She danced her way along the lane, golden curls tossing with each step, singing as she came, an unknown tune of her own making, as small children do, and calling "I've got a poppy for Betty". She stopped in front of me, offering her gift of one poppy and a quick bob that could have passed for a hurried curtsy, with all the confidence of the many little girls who present posies to Her Majesty The Queen. With a strange pricking sensation in my eye, I accepted the flower with as much graciousness as I could muster, though I doubt that it would have provided competition for Her Majesty!

We managed to transport this gift safely home in good condition, and it kept well in my specimen vase for a week – unusual length of time for a wild poppy.

Perhaps it was because this little girl had searched for the biggest example of a flower she knew I liked, or maybe it was just because she wanted to give me a flower anyway, or was it her simple pleasure in a simple gift, or was she prompted by an unseen hand to give me a precious moment that has stayed with me so clearly for all of twelve exciting years? I shall never know the answer, but I do know the result of that small child's kindly thought and action.

We must surely be grateful that we are sometimes given such great and lasting pleasures from such unsophisticated moments, but there are many in this world who seek their pleasures only in artificial circumstances or the raucous sounds of imitation happiness – that cost a lot of money – and must therefore be enjoyed to make the expense worthwhile. Meanwhile they miss the truly joyous, memorable moments that could so easily be theirs.

★ ★ ★ ★ ★

THE CIRCLE OF ALL LIFE

Everything of earthly life has its beginning and end in that particular form, but the end of earthly existence is the beginning of the next stage – the life after earthly death. Nothing escapes this circular principle of birth, death, and life again.

It manifests in the formation of the very rock, sand and soil on which we live on earth. It is a very obvious pattern amongst the vegetation around us. A seed drops from a plant, germinates, grows and flowers, and produces more seed to be dropped and continue the cycle of its own particular brand of life. As each tiny newborn tree grows, it too drops seed of its own kind, and also adds to the soil around it – its own leaves so that it can in turn nurture the seed and young life, for in nature nothing is wasted and everything has its use and is shared with other life around it. The combining ingredient of all life of every kind is Spirit, which has no beginning and no end, but rather is more likened to a continuous thread that binds each part into the whole.

Each kind of life has its own particular thread to suit its own existence, but when these links are woven into the pattern of Spiritual existence, we can perceive a truly glorious coat of many colours, too beautiful to describe in earthly terms, and yet all earthly life can accept its warm protection and comfort, for although Spirit is the distant vision, and emotional glimpse that promises a much greater and more wonderful experience, it is there for all to see who will, and all to know who wishes, for even the wayside flowers are part of the plan.

The spirit of the human soul sees and experiences such things according to its own knowledge, and those with greater knowledge can help others who are in need of it.

This greater knowledge may manifest in people of any age or circumstance, thus greater wisdom may be seen in the elderly or the young, depending on the spiritual experience of each person. Age guides with experience, faith and memory, whilst youth guides with hope, trust and a listening ear.

On the earthplane school, those who have lived there longest will have had the more time in which to gather spiritual knowledge amongst the practicabilities of earthly knowledge, but some younger people may have come to earth with greater spiritual knowledge than others, and be in a position to help other older folk, if they in turn are willing to learn.

It becomes abundantly clear, as the mind searches for truth and logical explanation of all things and all experience, that everything merely evolves and links one with another, everything depending on something else and giving to something else.

Like the trees with their seeds and leaves, giving to the earth and taking from it, people also come and go, giving and receiving and like the trees, age is of no importance. The older the tree the more fertilising leaves it has to offer, the more seed it can produce to further its kind and nourish surrounding wildlife, until in very old age when its earthly work declines it begins to wither. Eventually it has fewer leaves to offer and requires less for sustenance. Even then, in its slowing down, it offers shelter, food and its own kind of beauty to the other life around it.

When the human mind perceives the wonder of such planning and understands it in himself, using it to guide and help others of lesser spiritual knowledge, he becomes aware of the strength of the circle of all life, the glimpse of perfection reserved for those who truly wish to see.

The highly evolved spirit is the product of advanced spiritual knowledge, protected by true understanding of that knowledge. Such a soul gathers unto itself a small portion of the wisdom of God, and learns to understand its meaning. Together they embody the wisdom and understanding of Spirit, but separated the task is only half accomplished. Divided, each part fails to link and create the desired achievement, but when spiritual knowledge and understanding walk together as one, they are the supreme and complete circle of life in mankind.

SEPTEMBER GARDEN

There's nothing quite so beautiful
    As September's golden hue,
There's nothing quite like footprints
    In the morning's cool moist dew.

No other month brings mystery
    That filters through sun-rays,
The secrecy of morning mist
    Changing to golden days.

Jewelled cobwebs dry their threads
    From fiery leaves of heaven's tree,
Late summer daisies tumble down
    Cascading round the last sweet pea.

Walking down the silent paths,
    Hearing autumn's quiet cries,
By the sedum's rosy heads
    Through a cloud of butterflies.

Splash of orange, dash of red,
    The air is scattered with perfume,
That final thrust of energy
    From roses in their second bloom.

Twilight falling, autumn sun
  Dips his head in Holy Mass,
Shadows lengthen, tinged with blue
  And purple shades of Michaelmas.

CHILDREN IN MY LIFE

Children have not been a very specific part of my own life, my footsteps having taken me in other directions. Nevertheless those footsteps have at times walked with a child for a little while, or I have experienced some brief encounter that made a lasting impression. The little boy who climbed upon my lap, put his arms around my neck and said "I love you" for no apparent reason. The little girl of around five years, with her parents at a hotel table next to ours – so quietly charming, yet it seemed, too old for her tender years. She seemed to me to have some angelic wisdom behind those young and innocent eyes. I feared for her parents as I wondered if that little wise young life could be with them for any normal span, and I have often wondered what lay behind my own thoughts about her, and what was ahead for that very nice family, for the memory of the child remains with me so clearly.

How little we know of the influence and effect we can have on others – a timely reminder to try and make that influence to good purpose. We may never know the results of the effects we have on others, but by behaving, thinking and living to the highest standard that we can reach as often as we can, we can certainly help as many people as possible and harm fewer than we otherwise would.

Among the children I have walked with for a while, parted from and yet returned, there is my God-daughter Elizabeth, now a charming adult with two children of her own. Her parents were a nice and sensible couple of quite modest means, who succeeded in bringing her up along with a younger sister, to become this lovely lady of kindly disposition, helping everyone around her, following the teachings of her own faith, and presenting to the world two delightful little girls as sensibly brought up as she herself, and just as well mannered, a happy reflection on the grandparents, my friends.

Nothing unusual in any of that perhaps, but when I look around me at people of similar age to my God-daughter and at other children of the same age as her offspring, all with similar circumstances to their's, I can't help wondering at some of the extraordinary differences in the results of some of them. What really does make the difference between people who are a delight to know and the people who are not? when most things on the material level are more or less equal. Parents can be of similar nature basically with comparable standards of life and living, and yet in one family a child is a credit to its parents, in another a child appears to be difficult and wrong – even sometimes a burden that can cast a shadow on its family for a long time, possibly all their earthly lives. One can even see such a difference between two children in the same family without any obvious reason.

Sometimes there seems to be something deep within a child that makes it go wrong no matter what advantages he or she has had, or however much they have been loved and cared for. Sometimes the proverbial 'black sheep' of the family appears, (which perhaps is a little unkind to sheep of that colour) but it seems that in spite of every possible advantage, nothing can save such a child from the downward path and becoming worse with every detrimental experience. Some people can rise above every adversity and climb to the mountain top, whilst others could not even see the view from such a peak if they were placed there without any effort of their own. Indeed, perhaps it is the effort that helps appreciation. It seems that success or failure, kindness or cruelty, love or hate may be opposing experiences of the soul, brought to earth with earthly birth, rather than the result of incarnating experience.

I personally know a wonderful couple with a grown-up family that is a credit to them – except for one, who has become one of life's failures. With the aid of drink, drugs and a complete lack of consideration for others, plus a fair amount of laziness thrown in, this man – this child of successful, caring parents, appears to have this in-built determination to fail. His parents naturally wonder why, for surely there must be some hidden reason for such an apparently illogical situation.

I have some true and lovely friends in Yorkshire and I recall their eldest child when he was a baby. My main recollection of him at that time, surrounds the fact that he seemed to be always crying. Not yells of bad temper, nor the frightened squeal of pain, just apparently crying for the sake of it, for medical checks could find no cause.

These parents too came from that solid stock of humanity, sensible, kind and tolerant. Their second child wasn't like it although circumstances were the same, but the first one continued for some time to reject all offers and persuasion to keep him happy and well fed. His mother once said to me "It almost seems as if he doesn't want to be here sometimes". The phase departed in due course, as the smiling times began to outweigh the tearful ones, and he is now a successful geologist and respected academic, bringing up a happy family of his own, with no signs anywhere of that early worrying start. Whatever the cause, he somehow overcame it. Could he perhaps have come to earth with some in-built knowledge that faded with increasing age? Perhaps this particular soul fought and overcame a problem that came with him into earthly birth, while others fail.

It was many years later that I again came across another problem baby of close acquaintance. Again, sensible, caring parents with an elder daughter who showed no early problems. But the younger child was literally kicking against nearly everything he came across when he was in that sort of mood. No matter what these caring parents did to try and solve the problems for that little child, he seemed determined to kick out and challenge his world in any way he could, even if he did keep stubbing his toe in the process. There were many moments of baby charm and smiling delight of course, but if some of those smiles disguised an inner thought that he didn't dare to share, then we were left to guess, and in guessing we would have risked misunderstanding, and so such moments remained unresolved.

My husband Ken remarked on one occasion, that this little child seemed as if he resented coming to this earthplane and was kicking against it. Memory rang the bell, and I recalled my friend of many years expressing the same thought about her own baby son.

Because we were so concerned about this latest difficult child, we asked for Spirit healing for him and the reason for his unpredictable behaviour, bearing in mind his parents caring attitude and that his elder sister showed no signs of it. We did receive a Spirit reply, and an explanation that the soul of the child had chosen to go to earth to pay a karmic debt from a previous life. Having arrived at his earthly destination, that soul began to wish it hadn't, and was expressing resentment in ways that were in keeping with that earlier incarnation. We were assured that these memories which the soul had brought with it, would fade beyond earthly recall, that the child would be helped in his soul's self appointed task towards its own progression. This seems to be happening according to that indication and it remains to be seen what success he makes of his life. The signs are good so far, as a bright and active mind gradually replaces that sullen challenge to earthly life.

In recent years, much has been discovered, said and written about the allergic effect of certain chemicals in food, and even in natural unadulterated fruit and plants as a cause of some of the strange and even delinquent behaviour in both children and adults. Undoubtedly experiments with diet have shown that if certain substances are avoided, the behaviour pattern improves, often in a quite startling way. This seems to satisfy most people and it is as far as they want to go with this particular situation. But some of us will still ask why some children are allergic to these things, why their chemical make-up should be so different with such unhappy results, whilst their brothers and sisters remain unaffected in the same conditions and circumstances. It is worth noting that health and behaviour patterns can often be improved with different surrounding colours and even by the colours of wearing apparel. Quite extensive tests have shown this to be true, dark colours are known to be disadvantageous, whilst light and bright colours can help almost any condition. We have to continue to ask why, because otherwise there are too many questions left unnoticed and unanswered.

Perhaps in these physical conditions in which we live, the requirements of the soul have to be expressed in a physical way, with physical causes and effects. After all, if there are lessons to be learned in *this* life in order to overcome a condition of a previous one, or in preparation for the next, surely it is more than likely that it will have to be experienced in this way. In fact, how else *could* we learn in this world? It would certainly give a logical reason for someone to be exposed to these strange allergies, whilst others in similar circumstances are not. Perhaps a person's chemical make-up can be both a cause and effect of a soul condition.

It is quite clear that we all come here to this earthplane for specific purposes, most of us it seems, being given opportunities for the soul to learn and progress towards the infinite love and light of God. Some of us learn better than others, even as children in school vary in this endeavour. In life it seems that some do not learn at all, no matter what their conditions or advantages, yet it is quite easy to find highly evolved people who have risen from very adverse circumstances, shining examples that we can all be what we truly wish to be – spiritually speaking.

I began this chapter with some happy reminiscing. I will end it on the same smiling note, and must therefore tell you about Jane, a child in Spirit who chose us to tell of her experiences in the Spirit World. Her story is fully told in our previous book *I'm Jane*, but this narrative would be incomplete without her because of the joy she has brought us, and the influence she has had upon our lives.

Jane told us she was five years old when she first communicated in 1984 as we sat in a circle with two good friends. In a gentle Irish brogue she delighted us with a fairy tale about banshees, and sang for us in a piping little voice, "Twinkle twinkle little star". Later, with the help of her grandmother in Spirit, automatic writing was used to relate her story.

We still do not know why we were chosen for that particular task, but we feel now as we did then, honoured to have been of service, and privileged to have met Jane. For me her communications are a highlight amongst the children in my life. She was such a pleasure to know, and the fact of her spirit survival in such a heartwarming way, is certain to be of great comfort to many parents whose child has returned to Spirit. This alone is more than enough to make Jane the most joyous child meeting of my life.

Not far behind were the dandelions! It must be thirty years ago or thereabouts that I met a little fair haired girl in the park at Ilford in Essex. She was dancing around the flower beds, her curly hair bobbing to the rhythm of her dancing feet, and quite oblivious of my fascinated gaze.

At that particular time I was making a film called "The Flowering Year", and had conceived the idea of a dandelion seedhead blowing in the wind to symbolize the continuation of flower life – the seed cast upon the winds of chance to start again another flowering year. But I had not solved the problem of filming this idea successfully – until I saw this delightful little girl of perhaps three or four years of age.

Her mother agreed to my filming her daughter, and I took along several beautiful full headed dandelion 'clocks'. Small lips were pursed ready to blow hard, as she held the stalk firmly in a fairy hand. As she blew the seedhead as hard as little lungs could blow, my camera whirred and the final shots for my film were in the can, whilst a little girl had somehow whirled herself into a special place in my memory.

I cannot remember her name, and I believe that something prevented me from showing the finished film to her parents, my memory is vague on these details, but I remember so clearly, this little girl who danced into my life but briefly, and danced right out again – with a huff and a puff that sent my dandelion seeds flying away – somewhere there is a dandelion plant whose ancestor took to the air that day, recorded on my film.

Perhaps somewhere in the world there is a charming fair haired lady who has a vague memory of blowing dandelion clocks when she was very young for some strange lady with a camera. If memory rings a bell for her too, I hope she'll somehow know the pleasure she has given me through all these years.

As I look back I am grateful to these children in my life, for all of them have taught me much, helped me towards a greater understanding, and contributed a glow to my living. By writing about them here, perhaps they will help others too, so that even the failures will have fulfilled a purpose, even though it be without their earthly knowledge. Perhaps in some way that we do not yet comprehend, each soul will know, or later be enlightened on the full impact of their toils and laughter here on earth, and realise the way that Spirit can use each one of us to good purpose, whatever our age may be.

ANOTHER LOOK AT SERVICE

On 12th September, 1988, I suddenly felt the now familiar urge to write. Taking pen and a scrap pad of paper that was lying handy, and without the slightest knowledge of what I was about to write, I put the aforesaid pen to paper and produced in a very short time about half the following words of wisdom. I did not have any identification for my Spirit Communicator, neither was it complete I quickly realised on reading the material I had been given. I put it aside and had forgotten about it until the 27th of September, when I came across the scribbled lines and knew I had to complete it then and there – right in the middle of something quite different! The following is the completed piece:-

In serving mankind you serve Spirit. In serving Spirit you serve mankind, each compliments the other, and all is but a pathway to God. Spirit is God, God is Spirit, and mankind is part of Spirit – all are part of that greater power, strength and light. Mankind is the weakest link.

Whereas many are becoming enlightened and more aware of the Great Spirit and thereby strengthening this band of brothers, many others still flounder in the darkness of ignorance, thus holding back the earthplane conditions, and preventing progress towards a peaceful, happier world.

Those of darker thinking cannot rise above the confusion and sorrow of their own minds until they wish to do so. It is for the more enlightened to show the way by fine example, brandishing the torch of spiritual endeavour, thus illuminating the darker places with the light of truth and love. Those in Spirit, seeking to help the erring world, can only await the opportunities to serve mankind, and bear with patience the failures brought about by earthly indifference and opposition. Such negative thinking hinders the work of Spirit, but cannot ever destroy it, for the love of God is all powerful and can overcome all evil. Only mankind delays the process.

It is sad that the negation and opposition often comes from well meaning souls upon the earthplane who have misunderstood true religious teachings. Truth has become twisted through the ages by the wrong thinking and actions of a comparatively few souls, who, whilst on the earthplane, manipulated for their own purposes or failed to comprehend the truth when they saw it. Sometimes mere human weakness of nature or knowledge, prompts other souls to follow in the footsteps of stronger yet less moral leaders, failing to understand or recognise the light of truth, or perhaps fearful to follow an unknown track.

But there is no longer need to hide this light beneath the proverbial bushel. In most countries of the world, there is now sufficient freedom for the glorious message and light of God to be fully acclaimed, so that those with true knowledge may light the way, that others can follow as soon as they quicken to the desire for enlightenment, a loving truth that can be expressed and lived as service throughout each passing day.

This expression of loving truth must manifest in daily thought and action, towards all living things, towards the natural beauties that surround you – the environment that sustains all life upon the earthplane. Through this loving care, all service is to God, through Spirit, through mankind towards everlasting perfection.

You will not know that perfect state whilst living in earth conditions, for the planet earth is a place of learning, and while learning is a necessity for the human soul, it follows that there cannot be perfection there. Only when all knowledge is learnt and understood could there be such a supreme state of being, and this can only be with God. All others are on the ladders of learning, either upon the earthplane or at varying levels in the World of Spirit, towards that ultimate achievement.

Religion should be a daily living of kindly thought and action. It does not require divisions or labels, it requires merely service from the heart and mind. It does not need gold or jewels, simply a true love of that power we all call God, whether we are on the earthplane or in the realms of Spirit. By our own service to others, we all take ourselves nearer to that perfection, no matter where we are, who we are or what our understanding of God may be.

The following experience demonstrates so well the lessons of loving service. This memory flooded back to me in January 1990.

During the '60s I met a charming Jewish lady whose family before the war had been of considerable opulence and social standing in Europe. She told me how her sheltered existence had blinded her to much of the horror that was sweeping across the continent.

In due course the Nazi threat almost caught up with her. She received a warning to escape immediately, and such was the urgency of the situation that she could only grab her baby and run in her expensive high heeled shoes to join the refugees that tramped slowly along the road below.

She told me how they had given her warmer, more suitable clothes from their own meagre supply because she had no coat. Someone gave her shoes as hers were completely useless in such conditions. They shared such food and money as they had, because she had none of these things.

Tears glistened in her eyes as she explained how these people for whom she had never spared a thought, had saved her life and her baby son, taught her tricks of survival, the lesson of humility, the necessity of hope and the value of courage.

She and her baby survived only because of the kindness and basic love shown to her by people who appeared to have nothing. "It was I," she said –"who had nothing, and I had seemed to have everything. I had never shared my advantages when I had them with such people as those who trudged that road." But those unsung heroes had willingly shared the only things they had with a desperate woman and her child, in horrific circumstances.

The lesson here is obvious, and my Jewish acquaintance had learnt it a very hard way. Perhaps her story will remind someone somewhere how completely valueless material possession and thinking can be, and how valuable the gift of unselfish love and courage. It reminds us that these come in many guises, from all strata of wealth and position, for this lady in her turn, was able eventually to play her own part in helping her fellow travellers and give her own loving service to some of those who had given so generously to her, a perfect pattern of service to God through service to man.

AS AUTUMN COMES

The autumn mist will gently shroud the hills,
And hide the fields where summer's ploughman tills,
Or send clear waters gushing through the mills,
And silence reign where springtime's blackbird trills.

Golden leaves will toss and rustle as they will,
Autumn fruits will fall, their purpose to fulfil,
While butterflies will sleep and dream until
God's masterplan of nature serves us still.

★ ★ ★ ★ ★

SCATTERED WORDS OF WISDOM

My childhood memories of September, are chiefly concerned with masses of flowers, fruit and vegetables in church and Sunday School –of which I was a part – bringing the house down – so to speak – with enthusiastic renderings of "We plough the fields and scatter, the good seed on the land, where it is fed and watered by God's almighty hand".

My visualizations of the procedure at the time, were mainly concerned with the ploughman steering a team of majestic horses, and an angel-like figure of an elderly gentleman with a very large watering can. I don't think I imagined that this was actually God, more like His head gardener, who had been given his instructions and the can, by his heavenly employer who had a very large hand. All the best gardeners seemed old to me at the time, so it was appropriate enough to me for God's gardener to be of advanced years.

It did not of course take too long for my interpretation to alter and advance, but some childhood memories are very persistent, and this is one of mine. But although the picture becomes discarded and relegated to the attic of experience, the memory of it remains to teach further lessons whenever we choose to learn. With memories as strong as this one is to me, it is possible to use it all through one's life, as new occasions present themselves with new opportunities to glean and harvest the richness of early learning – those early seeds of wisdom.

For the benefit of anyone who may be interested in my own personal gleanings, I will relate some of my favourite memories that have frequently been of help to me one way or another.

My friend Paddy, who was for many years in charge of the animal ambulance service at the People's Dispensary for Sick Animals at Ilford, frequently and quite unconsciously shared her pearls of wisdom with others. Many an unsuspecting listener was startled by her sincere and uncomplicated philosophy, particularly where animals were concerned. My thoughts go back to an injured pigeon that could only hobble and flutter along sufficiently to escape capture, and was therefore unable to compete with the rest of the flock at lunchtime. Paddy went to busy Liverpool Street station in London in response to telephone appeals from the public for a rescue attempt, which she did in fact carry out with her usual calm efficiency.

As she was about to return to her ambulance with pigeon safely caged for the journey, an irate gentleman approached her and complained that it was disgraceful for the P.D.S.A. to use its funds on a mere pigeon when there was so much else to be done. Paddy's reply was a gem to me at the time, and has stood me in good stead ever since. "It can't help being a pigeon" was all she said as she quietly walked away.

How often do we walk away without even trying to do something to help, just because there seems to be something greater to do just ahead. Perhaps if we all attended to the more insignificant injustices around us, many of them would never have the opportunity to grow into the large almost uncontrollably bad situations that beset this world of ours.

It is also worthwhile remembering that everything has its use upon this earth, and its right to be here, and we should not perhaps condemn out of hand without more careful thought. This pigeon rescued by my friend, was one of a vast family of birds that have actually given good service to mankind. Apart from giving much pleasure and interest to many who breed, race and show them, the birds themselves have saved many human lives. In wartime in particular, pigeons have been released by airmen who have crashed into the sea. The amazing homing instincts of these birds have brought the message of the airman's whereabouts and subsequent rescue. Pigeons dropped by parachute into Europe during the Second World War to Resistance workers, were later released there to return to England with important information that could be despatched safely in no other way, saving lives and tortuous suffering. I know of one bird that carried out over thirty such journeys, arriving home safely with serious injuries at times.

In the First World War they were in common use to carry messages from the battlefront to base behind the lines, when other means of communication were non existent. It is quite impossible to estimate the number of human lives that have been saved by pigeons, or the amount of suffering that has been forestalled by these birds. And so, next time you find a pigeon eating your cabbages, or making some other nuisance of itself to our human way of thinking, remember, it can't help being a pigeon, and its distant relatives may have saved one of yours at some time or other. We may even require the homing services of a pigeon ourselves some day, perhaps our own lives could depend on one.

None of us can help being what we are or our circumstances of birth, but our achievements – good or bad – are our own.

My father had a number of favourite quotations that he liked to use from time to time, usually adding a little piece of his own wisdom. My own favourite is this: "Good deeds are like bread cast upon the waters, the tide will bring them back, but not always to the same beach from which they were cast". This valuable thought has stood me in good stead for many years. I have so often noticed that a good deed gets passed on to another and the perpetrator of the original deed never sees the result, but is the recipient of an entirely different form of help or kindness from some other quarter altogether. One is eventually left with the impression that someone, somewhere in the place that we call heaven, has a very efficient filing system, and in due time, every good deed is well rewarded. It is our own lack of understanding and patience that makes us feel thwarted and despairing when our own humble efforts appear to go unrecognised. We are told that God is always just, that His laws are perfect. If we believe in God, then surely we must accept this also, and look elsewhere for explanations when things seem to go wrong or kindly thought appears to go unrecognised. Possibly we are not looking in the right place, perhaps the tide of eternal grace has washed our bread of life upon another beach. Maybe we should look harder to find some kind consideration coming to us from an unexpected, hidden place, or perhaps we should not look at all, confident that our own kindly thoughts and actions will have their good effect where and when most needed, guided by the power and knowledge of Spirit. With this knowledge, we do not need to seek reward or acknowledgement, because, with this kind of faith, we know it will come to us sometime, somewhere.

Another mine of information and the scattered word of wisdom – James Cooper of the Renegades Theatre Company at Ilford. Through Jimmie, as he was known to his friends, I learnt some of the many words of wisdom that issued from the pen of William Shakespeare, and there are many that constitute wise counsel towards a better way of thought and life. But Jimmie had himself so much sound philosophy, and expressed it through his work and dedication in the theatre. This one simple fact is in itself a lesson that we could all learn to our advantage – to live our beliefs in our daily lives and occupations. But it is another small piece of his philosophy that stands out in my mind, a seed that was often scattered with the precision of a well ordered mind and the perfect timing of his profession. "Always aim high with everything you think and do," he used to say, adding – "You may not always reach your goal, but you will achieve much more than you would if your sights are set too low".

How very true this is, so few of us reach our real potential in life, usually because we do not aim high enough in the first place. We fail to understand the spiritual possibilities that we might achieve if we would only set our sights higher and make greater efforts towards our self-appointed goals.

By aiming high himself, this good friend achieved not only great moments of upliftment upon theatre's stage, but also on the stage of life and proved the truth of his own philosophy.

Many are those who aim high in the material sense, climbing ruthlessly through the jungle of human endeavour to acquire positions of wealth and power for its own sake. They even think they succeed as they survey the accumulation of worldly goods, the debris of their climb, their own inflated egos blinding them to the truth – they have climbed the wrong ladder, and having reached the top, find there is nowhere to go but down. There will be no shortage of aspirants ready to help them with the descent! Material achievement is only worthwhile if it is used towards good and unselfish purpose, that others in worse conditions and situations than ourselves may be helped.

The only worthwhile climb in life is for the achievements of the soul, the striving towards a better way of thinking and therefore better action. Using our physical position in life and material accomplishments, is merely a means towards our true goal, and not an end in itself. When we aim high towards spiritual achievement, we set our sights as high as is humanly possible. The results will therefore be the greater, even though we fail to reach perfection. As we glance back along the uphill path we have travelled, we shall see those we have helped, the flowers that bloom because of our own sowings of kindness and understanding.

Because we cannot reach perfection here upon the earthplane, there are always further heights to climb, always better views to behold and admire. No need to tumble from a pinnacle of spiritual achievement, for by aiming high we came prepared, and no one can dislodge us unless we choose to let them, for our knowledge is our protection, the rope that prevents the fall, and our understanding of that knowledge is our security. Our humility in achievement is our safeguard on the pathway that lies ahead.

Clearly our achievements in this life are not measured by an earthly yardstick – the worldly position that we occupy, but rather by the quality of the seeds we sow through life, the way in which we tend them and the harvests they produce. As my own memory turns full circle, I feel grateful for that early heavenly gardener of my mind, who taught me to plough the fields and scatter my seeds upon the fields of life. I am also grateful to those who scattered their own seeds of wisdom along my pathway, brightening my life with such masses of blossom, that my climb towards God is through an everlasting garden in all it's seasons, a garden of healing, peace and joy.

The foregoing memories of my friend James Cooper were written only a few days before he passed to Spirit. I have therefore very slightly adjusted the text. Shortly afterwards, I received from Spirit, a poem that I felt could only be a requiem for his life on earth. When a special memorial stage production was later organised by his wife Yvonne and some very good friends, I received a further Spirit poem, especially for this friend and lady of the stage, to help her at that difficult time. We know that Jimmie himself helped to inspire this second piece of verse, and my own mother helped him to communicate it. I offer both of these poems here with Yvonne's permission, that these words may be an inspiration and help to others, thus to demonstrate that the good we do in life is never lost, it moves like oscillations in the air, to live and thrive and influence future days.

A SPIRIT REQUIEM
(for Jimmie)

When genius locks out all but striving's best,
And loyalty assumes the guise of sacrifice,
The goals thus set are higher than the rest,
Achievements rising higher than the skies.

And we who touch the life of such a man,
And know the privilege of learning from the heart,
Salute the whole of God's creative plan,
To find theatre's place – a race apart.

A life full lived towards a great achievement,
Unstinting effort – even in adversity,
To bring a truth of life to entertainment
With dignified, theatrical integrity.

And so at last the earthly life is done,
The soul will smile and reap its just reward.
The spirit life of joy has just begun –
Last call – 'Curtain Up' to loud applause.

For Yvonne – Actress, Friend, and Lady of Courage.

Memory is an enchanted road
    That winds and dips through hill and vale,
Sees every dream of life unfold,
    We smile or weep along each trail.

Sometimes the smiles are heaven's joy,
    Sometimes they hide a tear.
Deep sorrow may the tears employ,
    Or as laughter may appear.

But as you tread the stage of life,
    And give it all you've got,
The memories blend in sacrifice,
    To the friend that we call God.

Our gifts of life we choose to use
    The best way that we may,
An urge inside we can't refuse,
    To light another's way.

For when our talents brightly shine,
    The glow spreads far and wide,
And others reap with passing time,
    The knowledge we confide.

For when a life is truly lived
　In truth and honesty,
Translating what the soul believes,
　It proves God's majesty.

And when the task on earth is done,
　And the curtain falls on a noble life,
The stage is set for another one,
　Free of sorrow, free of strife.

Friends will gather from afar,
　Joyful, singing all the way,
Welcoming the homing star,
　Curtain up – to a glorious play.

And so may we who hover here,
　Lonely for a little while,
Re-use those memories held so dear –
　"You're on" my leading lady – smile !

MILESTONES

Once you are over sixty years of age, it becomes easier to look back at your own particular milestones of life, assess their value and more importantly perhaps, evaluate the use to which we ourselves have put them.

The milestones point the way and we can choose to follow their indication, but sometimes our choice is to deviate from that path and try a different route – usually to our cost – for the lessons on that pathway can be harder ones to learn, but they have their uses in as much as, we will often be much less likely to forget them. It is worthwhile remembering that milestones also tell us where we have come from, for that too had much to teach us that should be stored for future use.

It is a peculiarity of the human race that we often choose to learn the hard way, which makes our milestones all the more important to us, as a means of helping us with the right decisions in life. We tend to keep the deviations to ourselves, which is often the wisest course, the knowledge gained being of unparalleled value to the present and the future when in our own hands, but possibly a hindrance to us in the hands of others.

But the milestones we have followed through life, also have their value to others beside ourselves, for other souls, by observation, can then recognise more easily wise indications for their own lives.

These milestones of life showing where the pathway suddenly turned in a different direction, are sometimes remembered by a traumatic, or simply sad event, sometimes by a happy laughter making situation, or more often by a mere trick of circumstances that could not be easily recognised as a milestone until viewed by hindsight.

Such a situation came to me in 1979, when it became necessary for me to move house from Ilford in Essex, but a dilemma arose – where to? Family reasons tossed me about on the seas of indecision. Two directions presented themselves, to the East Coast where my favourite Aunt Elsie already lived in a house that was too small, yet an area with which I was familiar and I liked, or to the South coast where my cousin Ivy already lived, also my father's friend Oscar. But this was an area with which I was totally unfamiliar.

Then came one of those moments when a milestone came into view, disguised on this occasion as a mediumistic lady. It was after the service at Barkingside church, and everyone happily drinking cups of tea and chatting together. I can't remember her name now, but clearly recall her face, and certainly will always be grateful to her. She apologised to me for intruding, and gave an accurate description of my favourite uncle and some other relatives, in order to convince me of the authenticity of her message from this uncle, because she said it was important. I remember even now her very words – "He is saying, go south – they want you to go south."

This lady had no knowledge of me or the circumstances I was in, so this unsolicited piece of advice rather shook me, as I was inclined to lean towards the more familiar East Coast.

I thanked the lady (not nearly enough I now realise) and decided to consult another medium to seek corroboration of the message. When I did so, her first words were, "I don't know what they are talking about, but they are saying – go south". In the face of this, I took my courage in both hands, and the three of us moved south near Christchurch in Dorset, my aunt, my father and I.

I had to leave behind my absorbing work with the Renegades Theatre Company, to which I have referred elsewhere in this book, friends and a number of relatives of whom I was fond, but I knew by then that I had to go. Our new home presented itself in a mysteriously magical way, the move went smoothly and I began to attend Christchurch Spiritualist Church.

This proved to be a second milestone in the same sequence of events. A parting shot from Norman as I said goodbye at the Barkingside Church, had advised me that a silver cross would be in the correct church for me, but the cross in the Christchurch church was made of wood, so I was a little uncertain until I accidentally discovered a silver cross in a box in an outside storeroom – I was in the right place!

The proof of this came when Ken and I met and subsequently married in that same church, because that was the beginning of our spiritual work together. This was the purpose for which we had been brought together. Neither of us could have accomplished our spirit books alone. The milestones of our lives had pointed the way to bring about the purposes and plans of Spirit.

The problem with milestones is undoubtedly the difficulty of recognising them at the time we first see them. But those who are conscious of Spirit guidance have the advantage of knowing they can seek help to follow the right pathway. Even so, no matter how much help is at hand, it is still necessary to be aware of it and to be able to interpret it in the right way. This is the task of intuition rather than the intelligence of the brain, because there are times in our lives when it is wiser to respond to our instincts, rather than the reasoning of worldly standards of thinking. It is also our own intuition which can tell us which system to use and when, for it is a mistake to leave all our decisions to Spirit guidance, we have to play our full part and be responsible for our personal choices and their results in earthly life, whilst being aware of this other most valuable source of guidance at the same time – not an easy task.

The ability to hear the sound of intuition, is the ability to recognise the voice of Spirit. The faith to act upon it, is the courage to follow the direction of the milestones of life.

OCTOBER GARDEN

With fiery red and brilliant shining gold,
We gaze with wondering sorrow to behold
Each straggling flower, striving to grow old
With dignity, before the earth grows cold.

The silent slowing down of summer glory,
Renews each year the truth of autumn's story,
To rest before the springtime comes so surely,
Which winter's meditation proves entirely.

Some tired leaves give of themselves to earth,
To feed the soil and giving new flowers birth,
To show the value of their dying worth,
And prove eternal life in next year's floral dearth.

The nipping teeth of early morning frost,
Or heap of leaves where whipping winds have tossed
The loveliness that grew and lived and lost,
All play their part and must not count the cost.

And so October wends its glorious way,
Untidily through every autumn day,
And with its shaggy garden tries to say,
The time is near to rest, renew and pray.

AUTUMN-TIME TRANQUILLITY

I stood there on my hillside vantage point and looked across the valley at the sheep so quietly grazing among the patchwork fields of green and tidy browning hedgerows. My gaze wandered to my right across the river, shrouded now in morning mist, hiding the houses and any activity there might have been on the other side. Wisps of river mist slipped silently across the fields, like ghostly spirits trying to take form and prove a real existence. My field of vision expanded then along the wooded hillside across the peaceful valley, taking in three birds on the skyline, flying in leisurely formation to some distant destination of their own.

The autumn gold, was I noticed, giving way to the browns and lacy patterns of woodland's winter sleep, and my eyes, now mesmerised by the beauty of the scene, wandered on to the glory of a pink and orange sunrise that in its dazzling brightness seemed to challenge the autumn leaves and woodland view that tried so hard to doze and rest after summer's bright activity.

Four isolated farmsteads snuggled in the dips and hollows of the hills, another braved the unprotected skyline where the trees gave way to fields and modern farming, or perhaps it always had been so.

And now the sun itself is rising above those rounded hills, so brightly that unshielded eyes can scarcely look, and I must wrinkle up my face to try and see, lest I miss a wondrous moment that I know will not last long. Yet there it is, a glory that streaks the clouds with many hues, clouds that here and there reveal the intense blue of far distant sky, that journeys on and on to sheer infinity.

Somewhere among this beauty, this artistry of God, is captured the mystery of time, of love and sanctity of Spirit, the silence of peace and all eternity. For a few precious moments, I know the truth of pure tranquillity.

★ ★ ★ ★ ★

CHANCE AND MINOR MYSTERY

When people think of mysteries they usually refer to situations such as the Bermuda Triangle, Stonehenge, perhaps a strange haunting of an old Rectory, or some more modern unexplained phenomena like U.F.O.'s. Yet millions of small mysteries occur to ordinary people all over our world during the course of daily living, that are given but cursory recognition – if any at all – and are labelled chance, coincidence or merely strange.

Just a little raking around amongst our collection of memories will reveal some of these apparently insignificant occurrences that seem to defy orthodox explanation and reason. And yet – on looking back and giving more searching thought to some of these occasions, we can often – by hindsight – see some logic to them, we can in the light of later events at least see a reason, which leaves us only with the mystery of 'how'. Perhaps we will not discover the answer to that until we reach the 'Other Side', or maybe, many years hence, scientists will be allowed to discover such explanations for the use of mankind upon the earthplane. Meanwhile we mere mortals can still marvel at these daily living mysteries, and use them to promote more philosophical thinking, by allowing such situations to mull around our minds and channel our thoughts towards more spiritual thinking. These tiny scraps of evidence, so often lightly brushed aside, can be very useful pointers to a better way of life and thought, and if we let them, they can be a constant reminder that we are never alone or uncared for. There is always help at hand, to guide us, cheer us and sustain us. How exasperating it must be to some of our friends in the Spirit World, when we ignore their greetings or toss aside the evidence that they go to so much trouble to give us.

I will relate a few of my own situations of chance and minor mystery, for many who read my words will recognise the outlines of some of their own experiences, some will ponder, perhaps for the first time on the possibility of a hidden mind at work to help them shape their lives and fulfil their destiny in the best possible way.

Two of the most wonderful friends that anyone could hope to have came to me via a series of 'chance' situations. It was War-Time forties, and I lived at the time on a small holding in the glorious green of the West Country. The house snuggled into the foot of a hill at the edge of the village. The Irish airman who rented the upstairs flatlet had been suddenly posted, and he and his wife had just vacated the rooms. My uncle, a semi-retired farmer who rented our field on the hillside at the back, sometimes called in to see me as he walked back to his own homestead with his filled milk cans hanging on his bicycle handlebars. Sometimes in due season he came with an offering of a huge mushroom he had just picked in the field – an added bonus to his company.

Over our cups of tea the idle chatter turned to my empty accommodation, and thus began the friendship that has not only stood the test of time but has matured and deepened with the passing years. For within three minutes of leaving my home, my uncle had met my future friend's husband, who, clad in his Air Force uniform, was wandering along the village street, wondering where on earth he would be able to find suitable accommodation for his wife of not long standing. This future friend reasoned that the elderly and obviously local gentleman might be just the person to know all that was going on in the village – certainly he might well know of any vacant rooms. He did of course, having only just left me!

The airman called on me immediately, and mutually agreeable arrangements were made. "That was a lucky chance encounter" he thought, and to be honest – so did I! But on reflection, there must have been some organisation behind this plan to bring us all together. First, the Irish airman had to be posted away beyond the reach of my flatlet at the right time. My uncle, not only had to be renting my field, but also his cows had to be there at that particular time, for they could easily have been in one of his other fields that were not so near to me. It had to be that particular day when he elected to call for a cup of tea and a chat. He had to leave at the precise time that he did in order to meet my future friend, who also had to be in the right place at the right time – half a minute later and they would almost certainly have missed each other. Finally the thought had to come that this friendly looking local might have some useful information. And what a fortunate chance that I had mentioned the vacancy over our teacups, frankly I wouldn't have expected my uncle to meet up with a meandering airman who was likely to stop him with such a request. All this takes no account of the train of events that took me to that house in the first place – but that is another story. This one is sufficient to raise the question of how many spirit helpers were involved in the organisation, and were they all working individually with one overseeing guide to correlate the various thoughts and actions? Or was there a happy, gleeful band working together to bring about a truly beautiful and lasting friendship? Who can say? But certainly they succeeded.

FRIENDSHIP TRUE

Some things there are in earthly life
That never die or fade away,
True friendship, free of strain and strife
Will stay the course with proof, to say
The love of friends survives the night
Of sorrow, leading to a glorious day.

If distance prove a part awhile,
Or problems stretch this silken thread,
Then truth in friendship brings a smile,
And darker thoughts are truly dead.
True friends negotiate the miles
When minds and hearts are kindly led.

And when our lives on earth are done,
Tasks completed, knowledge gained,
The love of friendship still will come,
Reaching out to heal all pain.
For friendship true will join as one,
An everlasting joy ingrained.

Amongst my minor mysteries I must tell you about the bean sprouts. I had planted the seeds in two small containers. One I put in the greenhouse so that it would begin to grow immediately, the other one I placed in the refrigerator, to hold back germination for a couple of days. When I took this second one out, it was placed temporarily on top of a vegetable rack, which was covered with a lid, and was opposite our back door and had to be passed in order to go through the outer door. Next day, en route to the greenhouse, I discovered they were missing, and assumed my husband had moved them, or even perhaps thrown them away, assuming them to be rubbish. But no he had seen the seeds there but hadn't touched them.

We searched high and low, even in silly places; which one is apt to do when trying to solve an unexplainable disappearance. We could only find the original greenhouse container, the refrigerated one seemed to have disappeared into thin air.

Two weeks later or thereabouts, I mentioned the incident to a mediumistic friend, after she had suddenly said to me, "You keep losing things don't you – and then they suddenly turn up again in some obvious place." I confirmed this, as it had happened on several occasions, with a variety of small objects. This friend explained that the culprit was a little girl called Rosemary, who, in her spiritual environment, found it great fun to play these little games with me, and the more I searched for the lost objects and rational explanations, the greater the fun for the child, who certainly meant no real harm.

My friend told me to go home, speak firmly but kindly to Rosemary, asking her to bring back my seeds. She did – just one week later, I went out to the greenhouse, passing the vegetable rack where the beans had been placed originally, and am positive there was nothing on the rack then except my gardening gloves, which I observed and made a mental note to collect next time. I returned to the kitchen with my watering can, filled it, and again went through the back door, to pick up my gloves in passing – there with my gloves, three weeks after being left on that rack, were the bean sprouts, still in the same container, on moist tissue, still in the slightly swollen state they were in when first left there. I thanked Rosemary, we grew the bean sprouts and ate them, but they didn't grow so tall as the first lot. Where had they been? How were they taken and brought back again? and how were they kept in the same condition for three weeks? It is easy to say they were dematerialized – but how? There is however one thing we do know.

Our little friend Rosemary was playing games and having fun! It does seem from all we hear through the Spirit World that the children really do enjoy themselves, and in their different way, so do the adults.

Again my mind returns to the late 1940s, before I was conscious of spiritual matters as such. I often noticed the round old fashioned brass door handles turning when there was no-one there to turn them. One of my Alsatian dogs had the habit of turning similar wooden door handles in order to open the door for herself, and I assumed she was attempting the same thing with the brass knob – until one day I realised that she was sitting beside me while the brass knob quietly turned. It occurred many times and there was never anyone on the other side. I never solved the mystery, but I did notice that although the dogs didn't seem to mind this curious little phenomenon, my cats hated it and would back away from the door with fur raised on their backs.

In later years, when my interest had been awakened, I remembered this strange little example of psychic phenomena, along with several other different unexplained occurrences of the same period. Together these served to stimulate my thinking and thus helped to open my mind to ever greater knowledge.

Many psychic and spiritual experiences later, we benefited from our latest psychic 'party piece' – demonstrated by those in Spirit who simply wanted to help us.

I had arranged to go to our local supermarket quite early one morning. But I couldn't find my bunch of keys. Not too strange you might think – people with bad memories or careless habits are doing it all the time. But I *knew* for absolute certain that on this occasion such an explanation could not apply.

We searched for twenty minutes, both of us going over and over the same ground. When we had finally given up and I had accepted my husband's car key, Ken had a last look round our 'Quiet Room' which we use for meditation and healing. There on the chair seat on which he had earlier been sitting was my bunch of keys. It was just not possible for them to have been there before.

Mystified but relieved, I went shopping, and whilst there, met a lady from our church who was able to help my little dog who had a broken leg that was not healing, and who was also able to help me with a health problem of my own. I was just about to go through the check-out, whereas she had just arrived. Had I not been delayed for more than 20 minutes by the incident of the keys that disappeared and then returned, I would certainly have missed this helpful lady. Our little dog could easily have lost a leg and I would certainly have been even more in need of this kind lady's help. We are quite convinced that spirit friends arranged the whole thing for our benefit, because so many things have happened to us that defy rational explanations, that we begin to be able to recognise the helping hand of Spirit when we see it. How could we be so ungracious as to deny it or fail to thank them?

Several years before I moved to the Bournemouth area in 1979 and later still re-married, I had a sitting with a medium in the Essex area. It was she who saw clairvoyantly, a strange little object that she thought might be a buckle. She drew on a piece of paper what it was like – something like a capital letter H. She did know that this object belonged to a monk who she said would help me in some future spiritual work, and that I would come across this sign during the course of it.

After I had moved and soon after re-married, the trance work on our first book began. My husband Ken recorded it, and I committed the material verbatim to paper – handwritten. For this purpose I kept a pen with the folder, an ordinary ballpoint supplied by Ken from a box of odds and ends he had collected over the years. I had been using it for some time before I noticed the faint pattern on the black barrel and yes, you've got there first – it was the pattern drawn years before by that Essex medium. I have kept it as my spiritual work pen ever since, and have in fact written these words with it. It is of added interest that I have since then, been told by several different mediums about the monk in Spirit who helps me with this work.

Many people would dismiss all this as unimportant trivia, but to those who know about these things, it is another example of Spirit's use of chance and minor mystery – the triviality that says to us, "Yes we are here, we know what you are doing and the opportunities that will come your way, we can prove it and help you." What more could I ask of a mere pen?

Another chance and minor mystery of our lives began in July 1975, not to us, but to Tim, a future friend whom we had not even met at that time. On impulse, Tim felt impelled to jump into his car, equipped with his razor and a packet of sandwiches and head south to the Christchurch area. A series of minor mysteries led him gently forward to his unknown destination. Following that inspirational trail as a naturalist follows the spoor of an animal in the snow, he eventually came to a bungalow that he just knew he had to buy. His wife Edna followed at his request, they bought the property and were thus in the right place at the right time to meet up with us at Christchurch Spiritualist Church at a later date.

With his extensive spiritual knowledge, he was able and willing to guide us through the unknown problems of a first spirit publication. Without that help and encouragement it is doubtful whether *Kaleidoscope Of Living Thoughts* would have been accomplished, and certainly not so successfully. It is therefore unlikely that *I'm Jane* or this our current offering would have appeared in print either. At a point when we were completely baffled, Tim was even able to produce for us the name of our publisher – Regency Press – through yet another series of extraordinary circumstances, each one leading on to the next.

These are classic examples of all the right people being in the right place at the right time, as a result of careful planning by those in Spirit who choose to do this kind of work. How they do it is beyond our imagination, that they can and do create these chances and minor mysteries is beyond dispute. It is we on earth that so often fail to take the opportunities they offer. Happily, this series of opportune occasions were recognised and followed by us all, with the end product of a rewarding friendship and a considerable number of Spirit communications that can help countless people. Spirit's Mission Accomplished, via chance and minor mystery? nay – perfect Spirit planning.

So often the minor unexpected happening becomes something of importance in our lives, its value only recognised by hindsight. So often today's little mysteries reveal great significance at a later date. Sometimes we find we have been protected, on other occasions we can recognise opportunities which we have missed or taken. There are many times when they merely alert us to a different knowledge, giving us opportunities to widen our horizons, or take a different pathway.

So many searching souls seek their evidence amongst the big

and spectacular happenings. So often there is proof of a guiding hand and loving help in the little everyday occurrences of life – if we would only pause to recognise and acknowledge them.

THE FORGIVING TOUCH

Everyone at some time in their lives will have been faced with the need to forgive. How hard this is when someone has administered a disservice to us, perhaps a very real unkindness, possibly an act that has culminated in disaster, maybe even the death of a loved one. Such acts between two people are as numerous as the pebbles on the beaches of the world. They are the basic cause of so much sorrow and pain, and are very hard to forgive.

Yet if we do not show understanding and forgiveness, we create yet another bad thought and act to add to the whole. Once we accept the truth of the power of thought, we can also realise the harm that our own wrong thinking can cause. It is a special kind of love that can overcome this type of wrong, this sickness of the soul that harms ourselves as much as it hurts our victim.

Charitable thinking seems in short supply in this world of ours, and the pace of living or in some cases even existing, often seems to dictate the need of a harsh outlook. We argue that we need to be hard and unforgiving in order to survive.

We fear that if we do not act harshly, others will think us weak, take advantage and behave harshly towards us, and so we become involved in a vicious circle of thought and action from which we find it hard to escape. Somewhere along the line of events, someone has to break the stranglehold of this encircling chain. The way to freedom is through forgiveness, but we can see how this becomes difficult because of our fears. We may fear the loss of position, finance or prestige. We may fear effects upon our own family or friends, possibly we could even fear for our health or lives in extreme circumstances. The longer such situations continue, the harder it becomes to make the first move.

As we ponder on these thoughts, we begin to realise the value of avoiding such situations in the first place, or having been involved by someone else's action, or even perhaps our own, taking immediate steps to put the matter right.

Fear so often enters its negative head, as we contemplate our proposed healing action. We may receive a rebuff that is hard to take and so delay the act itself. Time goes on, and our kindly thoughts become more difficult to put into action, and then perhaps another splendid opportunity is lost. Many of us will recognise this train of events. Some of us will regret our lack of action at the right time, and know increasing fear to take a belated one. In some cases, we may think it too late, that the chance has gone for ever.

This is not so. Once we recognise the fact of survival of the spirit after so-called death, we can realise that our thoughts can even be projected to the World of Spirit and be accepted by those who are in that other world. Obviously then, thoughts of forgiveness either to or from such beings are more than mere possibility. Indeed, a soul in Spirit may be awaiting your own forgiving thoughts before it can make progress. That soul can then experience the knowledge of gratitude, another necessity for Spiritual progression. And if the forgiving is coming in the opposite direction, the same principle will apply. We on the earthplane still, can easily be in need of forgiveness from a soul in Spirit. With the greater knowledge acquired there, they may now be very willing to forgive some indiscretion of the past on our own part.

This two way exchange of emotion and love, is such a valuable ingredient to happiness on both the personal level and on a world wide scale, that it can hardly be over estimated. If forgiveness can be accomplished between two worlds, then surely the easier task is to forgive during earthly life, and thus use a golden opportunity to set a good example there. The deeper we explore the subject, the more complicated it appears to become.

Already we see that forgiveness entails the experience of fear and the emotion of love, and when you begin to explore the ramifications of these, the main issue can very easily become lost in the tangles of our thoughts. Better to deal with the matter of forgiveness at its simplest level. Just offer it as a gift of love. You may not receive in return, you may not even have your gift accepted. It matters not, your act of forgiveness will still be of benefit at some later time and will be of immediate benefit to you.

Let bitterness be no part of your own life, but let this special kind of love be the greater part, and you will have added a great deal of good to the world around you, causing your own light of Spirit to shine ever brighter. This helps those in the World of Spirit to guide you, and by your own example, others will gain knowledge and some will try to emulate your principles. This is the pathway of spiritual thinking that can forge new tracks across untrodden ground, that others may see and follow, thus opening up a new and happier way of life for many.

Once upon a time we are told, a man died in agony upon a cross, not as a punishment for evil deeds done on earth, but because those in power were afraid of him, fearing the fine example that he set and the words of Spirit wisdom that he spoke.

During those hours of pain we are told that he prayed, not for deliverance from the indignity and suffering he was experiencing, but for his own executioners – "Forgive them Father, for they know not what they do". How many of his followers today could forgive in such a majestic way? How many can forgive even a humble slight or misunderstanding let alone the cruelty, pain and shame of an unfair execution? Perhaps our prayer today should be "Forgive *us* Father, for we know not what we do".

THIS AND THAT

As I sit here in the comfort of a bright and airy room and my own armchair, my mind begins to wander amongst a treasure house of thought – memories, reflections on them, the present and the future. I know that in a little while another hand will guide my own, helping me to record the thoughts that tumble to and fro – thoughts that my spirit friends can inspire within my own mind – thoughts that can help others to a calmer, more tranquil train of thinking for themselves.

With pen in hand, a folder full of blank pages, and two Yorkshire terriers on my knee, my lap at least is full.

I am filled with wonder at the scene before me. The patchwork of green fields across the valley, with their thick neatly cut hedges, have a peacefulness all their own, where sheep may safely graze, and almost daily do so. Looking across to the wooded hill of skyline timber, our own hillside home gives an almost birds-eye view of the cows grazing in the meadows below and the curlews sweeping down to gather their own harvest of food. Across the tops of the shrubs in our own garden, I can see the River Torridge to my right, often with strange and beautiful patterns on the sandbanks when the tide is out, but now reflecting the blue of a clear October sky which could well compete with the blue of Mediterranean waters. Across the river is Bideford's cluster of houses, other people's homes – and I pause to wonder what is happening within those dolls house walls, for that is how they look from here. No doubt the occupants can see our own dolls house, if they have time and inclination to pause and gaze out of their own windows.

Late roses are nodding their heads in the breeze along the edge of the patio, and greenfinches, chaffinches and a single robin assuage their appetites at our bird table, confident that we will not hurt them. A bluetit taps happily at the nuts above the table, and an immature greenfinch watches hopefully for any small bits of nut the tit may drop. The youngster's mother being more adventurous and knowledgeable, clings to the nutcage herself and slyly drops a piece or two. A pair of wrens pop in and out of the bushes, content to pick up the softer food that others in their haste have dropped. Earlier a considerable flock of gulls worked their way up the valley from the sea, no doubt to find easier pickings on some inland lake or rubbish dump. This evening they will return, working the valley fields, accompanied by an oyster catcher or two, and will finally fly away to I know not where for their nightly roost. Somehow this daily behaviour pattern of the gulls reminds me of the pattern of life of people, except that gulls do not allow life to get so complicated as do their human counterparts.

Anchored yachts are bobbing on the water, and a small ship from some more distant place is ploughing its way upriver to discharge its modest cargo, and perhaps take on something else in place. Men will throw the ropes, lift and haul, while another sits high up driving the quayside crane. They will grumble and laugh, swear and hope that nothing will go seriously wrong, working through the day just like the gulls, and for the same purpose – survival.

Amongst the busy, sweating workers will be some who in their quieter moments may consider too the possibility of survival of the spirit. A few will know, some more will wonder, whilst others dismiss the possibility out of hand. They are an isolated small example of thinking the world over, yet they only have to look around them at the beauty of this place, to know that there simply has to be a God – an all powerful, all wise mind beyond our own comprehension, to have created all this. What purpose would there be in all this wonder, if our own existence ended here with death?

With every turn of the head in such a place as this, we see the lessons of God's plan, a spiritual curriculum for those of us who wish to learn. We know that every child has to go to school in this modern world of ours, we also know that you cannot force the child to learn if it does not wish to do so. We know too that some children learn much quicker than others. Some use the knowledge gained to good purpose in later life, whilst others will waste the education they have been given. In the school and university of life too, people vary in their ability to learn, their desire for knowledge and the willingness to use it well. It is in this realisation that we have to accept eventually, that there would be no point in our learning unless there is in fact a life beyond so-called death. Simple straight forward logic dictates that there must be a God, a perfect plan, scope for learning and opportunities to use the knowledge gained, which could be used both now and in an existence after earthly life. This must be so if anything is ever to make sense.

The nature of that life has been indicated many times by those in the World of Spirit who have been able to communicate with us here on earth. But many who do not accept that those in Spirit can make such communication, elect to choose their own idea of the nature of life after death. It is of little consequence. In due course, when the time is right for each of us, we will all find out for ourselves the truth of survival, and the nature of it, and as long as we have tried sincerely to live our lives in truth according to our own knowledge, all will be well. If we prove to have been misguided in our understanding and beliefs, we will have ample opportunity to adjust our souls to the real truth. Our only real cause for regret might be if we have on earth deliberately misled others into a wrong channel of thinking when we ourselves should have known better. The abundance of material available to us to guide us to logical and honest thought and action, leaves us without any real excuse for ignoring or distorting it to suit ourselves.

Too often we ignore the obvious because of misinformed doctrination. Too often our proper sense of values is polluted and even destroyed by the fashion of the moment, or the gimmicky thinking of disreputable 'salesmen of words' who care nothing for their product or customer, only being concerned for their own material gain, their personal position in earthly life. It is for us to contemplate the 'goods' they offer and assess their true value. It is our own prerogative to choose aright or squander our earthly and spiritual opportunities on false concepts. The right choice is often not the easy route. God has not promised us calm untroubled waters. He has promised protection, guidance and love to all who sincerely seek them, and demonstrates the perfection of these, with the beauties and gifts with which He surrounds us. We may have to search to find such gifts, but we must remember that we would not recognise the beautiful unless we could also see the ugly for comparison.

Early in the year we explored some of the lanes and byways of our area, a habit that has continued throughout the year. We found amongst the nettles, thorns and docks of the roadside verges, banks of primroses, lifting pale gold faces to the sun, where clusters of snowdrops had earlier braved the frost. As primroses faded, bluebells massed their trembling flowers or bravely stood in isolation. Red campion mixed their colours with the blue, awaiting foxgloves in their turn. Then valarian tumbled from drystone walls and clothed unsightly banks with bunches of tiny scented flowers, just as once they had disguised the ravages of wartime bombs and earned a second name of London Bombsite Weed, bearing their flowers like campaign medals for duty well performed. Here and there we saw wild orchids, standing firmly erect, challenging the passer–by to miss them because they are not expected. Later still bright red poppies shook out their dainty petals, for all the world like scarlet butterflies, and wild roses and honeysuckle drenched the air with perfume, drawing attention to the bramble flowers that later on will give fruit for the picker who is determined enough to brave the prickled branches. These privileges are there for all to see, but only those who wish to find will register the presence of such illustrious company, and really know the true worth of nature's gifts of beauty.

I watch a pair of buzzards flying to and fro, working the valley for their food. A magpie in the garden, smart and beautiful in black and white array, chases off a smaller weaker bird that must find sustenance at some other place. The sheep that graze so peacefully will eventually leave the field that is their sanctuary, and find themselves herded into vans towards the slaughterhouse, because mankind, preening his exotic power, reminiscent of the garden magpie, wishes to take the sheep for food, even as the buzzards fly and ride the thermals in their bid for breakfast. But then, they and their magpie contemporaries know no better, or any other means of livelihood, so perhaps we should not criticise them, it is us humans who have the knowledge for better, kinder living, and so often fail.

And so I sit here with this beauty all around me and have to accept that nothing on this earth is perfect, the best is spoilt by something ugly or only second rate, and the imperfections are not God's work, but man's. We it is who spoil and denigrate in our ignorance. We are also the ones who can preserve and foster the beauties of life, the good and worthy causes, and benefit ourselves so much in the process.

ON WINGS OF THOUGHT

The following are pieces of automatic or inspirational writing that came on several different dates, but which on closer inspection fitted together to make a satisfactory and rather different whole.

Readers may find it of interest to know that the first poem was received early in October, 1984, whilst the 'Sharing Loving Thought' poem arrived on two separate occasions – verses one and two on June 1st, 1984, and verses three and four on 7th November the same year, and the title of this one was given even later.

Most of the main piece (When Thoughts Go Wrong), was received in March 1989, but one part of it came on 30th October, 1984, and this has been inserted. These strange little anomalies show us yet again the amazing way in which Spirit can work with us and use us if we so wish, because all were written independently of each other, without the writer remembering or referring to the older writings. These all came to light whilst searching among collections of older material for this book.

A CALL TO STRONGER SOULS

Bring joy you happy heart
To those in need of peace,
Let understanding hope impart,
That sorrows quickly cease.

Bring hope you hopeful soul
To those who need your strength,
Let love be your supporting role,
To guide at greater length.

Bring love you loving mind
To light the lonely path,
Be loving true and kind,
To claim sweet peace at last.

WHEN THOUGHTS GO WRONG

How very easy it is to slip into the quagmires of life upon the
earthplane – those inviting patches of luscious green that seem to
promise every worldly pleasure – only to find they are traps for the
unwary. The more you try to extricate yourself from these clinging
boggy conditions, the more they seem to hold you, one ill advised
action leading to another, creating a vicious circle from which there
seems to be no escape.

The victim finds no comfort in the fact that his position is of his own
making, indeed he will rarely admit that it is, for pride will prevent
him doing so. If only such a person could acquire a little
spiritual knowledge and realise that all was not lost, much
sorrow – even despair would be avoided, for all that is required
is the realisation of conscience and personal regret. Sincere regret
for wrong thought and action automatically gives spirit guides
and helpers the opportunity for which they have been waiting, to
contact and influence that soul towards better circumstances. Help is
always at hand for those who truly wish for it – with and for the right
reason. That reason is an acknowledgement of the mistake and sincere
regret for it. There is no other way of opening the door for help to
enter.

The levels of mistaken thought and action vary from modest unkind
thinking to very dark, evil action, which of course begins with dark
thinking – the one follows the other, and in its turn promotes further
dark thoughts and often additional dark action – a vicious circle in
every sense. No aspect of wrong is too small or too large for Spirit to
assist in it's overcoming.

Healing prayer can often bring about the initial desire to overcome
wrong thinking and action in another soul. By the process of projecting
love in the form of healing thoughts on behalf of that person in need,

conditions around them can be sufficiently improved for Spirit to begin work through the conscience of the erring soul.

Spirit healing is not merely for restoring a physical body to good health, its primary purpose is the healing of the soul, which *can* be accomplished through healing of the body, but in the kind of soul discord and sickness of which we are speaking here, a direct healing can begin with a sincere and loving healing prayer which will start a train of events that can open up tremendous opportunities for good. Such prayers are but healing thoughts that can wing their way in any direction for any distance. If such prayer appears to fail, it is only because the intended recipient does not wish to receive it at that time. He or she may well become conscious of it at some future time and be able to respond, for kindly thoughts are never lost.

Spirit power will often use an incarnating soul to help another in these matters of wrong doing and thinking. In choosing the right person for any given situation, the opportunity arises for that person to advance their own soul's progress in spiritual matters whilst helping the person in need. The chance to act arrives, to be accepted or refused according to their own will.

This is one example of the circle of all life, the way in which God has created our very existence so that each soul, each personality, each situation, revolves around another, procuring as it goes, a constant interchange and dependence, where guidance, understanding, gratitude and knowledge are interwoven into a tapestry of life. It is for each individual to choose the threads they use and the picture they create. The end product can be beautiful, horrific, or any stage between. Love is the common denominator here, that can rescue any situation and create to perfection. It can enable a willing soul to give or an erring soul to receive. It forgives, it waits and encourages. It smiles or sometimes frowns, but has no selfish motive.

The love of Spirit never leaves the incarnating soul, no matter whether that soul shines brightly with the light of it's own progression, or wallows in the darkness of it's own fear, sorrow, ignorance or actual evil.

The influence that spiritual love can have, depends very much upon the willingness of the soul to receive it. If you close the door to offered help, whether it be from earthly source or Spirit offering, you cannot expect to benefit from the proffered loving help – it is behind the door.

But you have only to open that door in invitation to find the light of love waiting patiently to enter, to brighten your whole life, all your thinking, with warming healing rays of Spirit love and guidance that flies to you on wings of thought. When thoughts go wrong, this is the knowledge that makes them right.

SHARING LOVING THOUGHT

The peaceful love of spirits tending
Anxious souls on mother earth,
Brings the hope that they are lending
To every child of earthly birth.

If your sky is dark and gloomy,
If your feet slip on the rocks,
Take the hand of hope, and truly
Trust that God will lead His flocks.

But if your sky is bright and sunny,
Shining like a bright mid-day,
Share your feast of milk and honey
With those who pass along your way.

Thus the happy deeds of kindness
Multiply and wander far,
Cheering, clearing all the sadness,
Twinkling with the brightest star.

A MATTER OF CHOICE

The power of thought is supreme in strength and gentleness. It can bring about that which seems miraculous, or guide along the gentle pathways of compassion. It can move material objects or the searching soul towards God.

Thought, being the prerequisite of action, prompts kindness or cruelty, love or hate, it is the individual who chooses the direction that thought will take. It may not always be possible to control a particular thought from entering the mind, for that thought may come from an outside source, but it is infinitely possible to govern its development and channel it into action for good or bad. Herein lies the opportunity for the soul's freewill.

Here is the moment of truth – when thoughts are sent out to wing their way towards the Spirit Power of love and compassion, – unless a different target is chosen. It is for each individual to choose, and the choice will determine the progression of the soul. Let loving peace encircle the world on wings of thought, the symbolic dove of peace.

NOVEMBER

NOVEMBER GARDEN

November's garden rests awhile,
Untidily she hides her smile
In knowing summer's task is done,
And rest will come for every one
Of nature's plants and fine display,
That lifted hearts with fine array
Through all the months of recent past,
To bring them peace and rest at last.

Crumpled leaves of brown and grey,
Give their life to a future day,
When flowers will reign supreme once more,
Nurtured by this silent store
Of nature's own recycling food,
To reawaken springtime's mood,
And follow with all summer's splendour.
November feeds that great endeavour.

Summer songsters flown away,
The garden silent of their lay.
Sharpening frosts break down the soil,
And winter winds resume their toil
Of pruning out the weaker branch,
And stripping leaves to thus enhance
Next year's dress of springtime green,
The finest gown you 'ere have seen.

The last of Autumn's fading flowers,
Contribute life from summer bowers
In gentle modest sacrifice,
To next year's floral paradise.
November takes these gifts of life,
Refashions with her natural knife,
To bring the glory of next year,
When love and beauty reappear.

So if your task in life is hard,
And you can see no quick reward,
Perhaps you are November's child,
Toiling through the winter's wild
And twirling winds, that garden more
Than all the effort spent before.
So when your summer buds unfold,
Be thankful for November's cold.

GIFTS OF THE SPIRIT

The following is another trance communication from "Friend", which
he called Gifts Of The Spirit, and was brought to us on two separate
occasions, 3rd February and the 9th May, 1989.

It is noteworthy that the two pieces dovetail together in spite of the time lapse, and the fact that there was no reference to the first communication between the two dates on the part of the Medium. It is quite impossible to know whether "Friend" himself referred to the first part before communicating the second, but it would be a normal and acceptable thing to do in his case, whereas it would not be acceptable for the Medium to have done so.

Once again we find him using flowers in a symbolic way in order to make his teaching more readily understood.

Gifts of the Spirit may be compared to the perfume of flowers. They are as varied in kind, strength and purpose. You cannot touch these gifts, even as you cannot touch the perfume that issues from the flowers of your earthplane. You cannot see them, you can only see the results that they bring. They are as subtle as these perfumes, and their cause is as much hidden from earthplane knowledge.

The most usually recognised gifts of the Spirit are your clairvoyance, clairaudience and clairsentience – but friends, there are many, many more. The wonders of gifts of the Spirit defy explanation upon the earthplane. Your scientists seek to find, and so far they fail, partly because they seek in the wrong direction, partly from the wrong motive and partly because there is usually more than one explanation, and these multiples have to be amalgamated in the right way. But for the most part, the reason for failure is that mankind is not yet ready to know such answers.

They will be revealed in due time, but history reveals that too many people will abuse that knowledge, they are not ready. In speaking of abusement, we should here point out that even as the perfume of the flowers can be sweet and beautiful, bold, sharp and scintillating or occasionally unpleasant, so the manifestation of gifts of the Spirit varies in such ways. Your sweetly scented violets, so shyly hiding in your hedgerows, can scarce be compared with the bold perfumes of some of your garden flowers, which it should be remembered, have evolved from the simple wild flowers with the help of earth's gardeners who have this particular gift.

There are also the entities on our side of life who exhibit the darker thoughts and unpleasant perfumes. The smell of evil is obnoxious indeed, and there are those upon the spirit lower levels, who try to influence people of like mind on the earthplane. Some people may wonder why those of us in the Spirit World, do not influence those darker minds and prevent them from – in their turn – influencing those upon the earth. One reason is that the soul upon the earthplane sometimes is unevolved and welcomes such influence, and we are powerless to prevent it while that soul prefers darkness. Some spirit entities work very near the earthplane, most for good, but a few for ill intent. These are beyond the help of those in Spirit with the knowledge to assist them, for again, those entities must experience the wish to grow away from their darkness before we can help them. Always remember that gifts of the Spirit can seem two sided, for there are many who will misuse these gifts even as they misuse some of the beauties upon your earthplane, so that your environment suffers, other people and animals suffer because of this abuse.

Gifts of the Spirit are bright and beautiful for those who wish to know them and use them well. It is misuse that darkens them and spoils their beauty until restored by truth and enlightenment.

Those with a particularly musical ear may be able to write much beautiful music, or interpret the music written by others. These are gifts of the Spirit. Some may be able to express much beauty with a paint brush and colour upon a canvas. In both cases much beauty can evolve, but beware discordant notes that jar the harmony. Beware the ugly or clashing violent colours that portray dark thoughts, possibly within the mind and soul of the artist, or the mind and soul of the spirit who uses him. I use these two examples so that you may see how a wonderful gift can be used for good or ill. The freewill given to all upon the earthplane can choose between the one and the other. It is good that those who recognise the brighter purity of good Spirit, should help others to do the same, and fight the darker forces that seek to influence through such channels – a special form of healing.

Many people have a gift of words which they can use with speech or pen and paper. They can use them to comfort and help those in trouble and sorrow. They have a gentle understanding of the World of Spirit and love of God, and use these gifts to uplift and lend courage. If such gifts are misused they can only hurt and destroy.

The greatest gift of the Spirit is the gift of healing. To be a channel for Spirit to heal the sick of mind, body and soul is the greatest privilege, because it gives us the opportunity to help those who are in need of progress for the spirit, towards the greater light of God, and those upon the earthplane who are the instruments of this spiritual work have a gift indeed and a special responsibility. It is not always realised that the gift of healing is not merely the laying on of hands accompanied by prayerful words. That prayer must be in attunement with the healing power. Many people can be used to heal, particularly with words. Those that have the gift of comforting the sorrowing, those that can uplift with words and those that have the gift of guiding on to a better pathway of thought. These too are healers of a slightly different kind, so that it can be seen that healing is part of all other gifts as well as the specialised task which each of those performs. The clairvoyant can for example heal with words from Spirit and many others who would not claim any psychic or spiritual gifts at all, are nevertheless influenced to give if they are sensitive enough to receive. They in turn can pass the word of Spirit on. There is no name, no recognition for these gifts, but they are there in daily use.

The most important part of healing is the healing of the soul. There are so many on the earthplane in need of this healing, and usually they do not recognise the fact that they are in need. They blunder on through life spreading their despondency or cruelty, perhaps selfishness and greed or lust for power, and do not realise they are the instruments of the darker forces who forever seek to dominate. But those who know the truth of light and love, must continue to pursue the higher ideals, their task in life on earth. We will support them in all they do, in all they think and feel. It may sometimes be thought that small contributions do not count and have little value. But they do, for as you know, even as your oceans are made up of tiny drops of water, so the wonder and power of God, the beauty and strength of Spirit, is made up of many small proportions of good and love and light, and together they make a tremendous power that can easily overcome the evils of the world. It is the need for more souls upon the earthplane to recognise their own healing power, their own potential for spreading the light and love of God. In His wisdom He has made man so that only he or she who is ready can recognise the need, and recognise their own ability to add their own small portion to the whole. It is part of the evolution of man.

Remember friends that every kindly deed you see, every kindly thought of which you know adds to the power that can overcome evil on the earthplane. Never let despair enter into the mind, for this is negative thinking. Always know that for every dark deed, every evil thought, there are more and greater thoughts for good, which culminate in action for good deeds towards perfection.

Remember too, the power of healing comes from Spirit. We ask that each of you in your own particular way, seek to become the channels by which healing can be administered to your world. When gloom and doom seems to be too strong, you only need to lift your minds to a higher level above the mists of darkness, and use your memories to picture all the beautiful things that are in your world, and you will realise that there is more beauty than there is darkness. Think upon these things my friends, whatever your gift may be – to write, to sing, to draw, to speak to comfort, and uphold the beauties of your world, the preservation of good things that mankind in his foolishness has put in jeopardy – these things are all part of the gifts of the spirit and the healing power of God. Remember these things and you can add your portion to overcome all darkness.

Gifts of the Spirit have been given to you to use well, and it is for you to accept those gifts and the challenge that they bring to use them with love and compassion. That is the pathway to peace and eventual happiness. It is your road to God.

★ ★ ★ ★ ★

THE COMING OF WINTER

Nature now prepares her winter sleep,
Spreads her leaves, the summer warmth to keep
And make the bed for blanket snows so deep,
To cosset the plants as to their rest they creep.

Spring buds are neatly tucked away,
To weather the storms of a winter day,
And nestle themselves from the wild affray,
Keeping harsh winter gales at bay.

Red autumn berries greet the frost,
To say that summer will not be lost,
But merely sleep in branches tossed
By winter's wild and windy host.

And so God's winter settles down,
To rest the world's poor worried frown,
Yet from that sombre white and brown
Creates a perfect rainbow gown.

For while all nature dozes in her rest,
And sunny days are just a welcome guest,
We know that spring will come with joy and zest,
To clothe the land again with all thats best.

★ ★ ★ ★ ★

THE ANIMAL KINGDOM

Many and varied are the views on the subject of pet animals. Some people upon the earthplane have no interest at all in animals or wildlife of any kind, apart possibly from their actual use to mankind, particularly as a means of monetary gain.

This is a very unevolved way of thinking, and all who care about animals, wherever they may be in the world, should take any steps they can to improve this situation, from the point of view of the animals themselves, and also those who harbour this archaic way of thinking, because it will certainly hold back the progression of such a soul.

Even people who could not actually and intentionally harm an animal, may not have any *true* feeling towards the animal kingdom. This section of the community can be readily recognised by their lack of support for animal causes, as they believe that while there is so much to be done for the human race, little time or resources should be used for the protection of animals. Some such persons actually keep animals as pets perhaps, or for leisure or pastime pursuits, and keep them in good condition physically. But this is not enough. Such owners may be keeping their animals for a variety of wrong reasons, which all amount to one thing – they use their animals to sustain or inflate their own egos, and this is not right in any field of endeavour. For the most part the animal will not suffer physically, but the soul of the owner certainly will spiritually.

It should always be remembered that where there is life, there is some kind of aura and some degree of spirit influence. The degree of this influence depends entirely on the degree of evolvement of the individual life.

This applies to mankind himself, every individual person is on his own particular ladder of spiritual achievement, and it can be quite clearly seen by anyone who observes the varying standards of kindness and understanding amongst his or her fellow travellers. The same principle applies to all animal life.

Even amongst wild animals it is possible to observe a more kindly nature in some than others, and this becomes even more obvious amongst domestic animals. When you begin to look closely at pet animals, it becomes abundantly clear that some are much more evolved spiritually than others.

With this in mind, it also becomes clear that the human race, which has greatly helped to bring this situation about, by domesticating the animals for its own purposes, has a duty to respect and nurture these animals as they would a fellow human being. Man, by his own actions through the ages, has made himself responsible for the animals who share the planet with him.

Even on a purely physical level this should be obvious, because if the animal has flesh, blood and a nervous system, it is capable of feeling pain and fear, and no-one has the right to inflict pain or fear on others. When they do, they are creating a karmic debt that one day must be paid, or life's accounts would not balance, and each must pursue their own endeavours until they do.

Fortunately, there are many people who, although keeping animals for some purpose other than purely as pets, do have an understanding of their true station in life, and the relationship between the two becomes a happy working partnership – a sharing – that can also happen between two people, and very often does. This demonstrates the knowledge of an equality of life and purpose that presents a fine example to an erring world.

There is room to consider that animals can in some respects, be more evolved than some of their human counterparts. The animals for instance do not normally inflict suffering or kill for the sake of it, or for any personal gain, other than the necessity to eat. Yet some members of the human race kill and maim because of greed, for the purposes of a lust for power, revenge, intolerance of other races and religions, envy and hatred. Animals do not exhibit any of these, not even the wild animals of the world. These facts should certainly give food for thought, and the human being should by now have progressed far beyond this state of thinking.

Anyone who has enquired to any extent into the facts of survival of the spirit after earthly death, will have discovered that animals also survive, and much evidence has been brought to you from the World of Spirit to prove it to be so. Not only that, but those animals that have lived in the same conditions as their human companions upon the earthplane, occupy a similar place in Spirit, being cared for by loved ones. And if they had a particular task or pleasure on earth, they will continue to exhibit it on the Other Side.

Those who know the trauma of losing a much loved pet animal, will inevitably grieve for a while because of the loss of that physical presence, as they would grieve for the loss of a human companion that they loved. But grief should never last too long, because it holds back the spirit of the one who has passed on to the next sphere of life.

Anyone who has truly loved a pet animal, will know how sensitive it can become to your own thoughts and feelings. If you for any reason feel unhappy, your pet becomes conscious of this, and millions of pet owners can testify to the sympathy expressed to them by an animal. It becomes obvious, that just because a pet has passed to Spirit, it will not lose this ability any more than would a human counterpart. It behoves all pet owners then, who have loved and lost their earthly companion in the physical sense, to let their pet be happy in their new surroundings and not let grief sadden a wonderful new life. Someone it knows and cares about will be looking after it, and it will also often be around you and sharing still your own life. This has been demonstrated by Spirit so often, that it cannot be denied. So those of you who grieve for a pet, grieve not – the pet is there and loves you still, and will have opportunities to progress. If you loved them enough on the earthplane to make them happy then, you can love them enough to make them happy in the World of Spirit.

Miss them you certainly will, but the memories you hold dear should not sadden you for too long, but lift you up towards happier thinking. Their earthly lives may be short compared with that of the human race, perhaps they need less time than us to accomplish their earthly tasks. We can only be grateful that these souls of pet animals have been lent to us for a little while, that we may have the privilege of loving them and caring for them, learning from them and teaching them. They have a right to be happy in the Spirit World just as they have the same right to happiness on the earthplane, and it is up to us owners to make sure we give them that opportunity.

Take comfort in the presence of the pets you love, enjoy that presence to the full, whether it be on the earthplane or in the World of Spirit. Your love will be well rewarded, your memories will sustain you – and them.

A PRAYER
WHEN A LOVED PET DIES

Lord bear with me because I grieve,
I'm lonely for a little while.
May your blessing I receive
To help me travel this dark mile.

I thank you for the life you lent,
To cheer the road I've trod,
That little soul was heaven sent,
And brought me nearer to you, God.

I've done the best I can oh Lord,
To care for this small soul for you,
I give it back with gratitude
And love that's kind and true.

I know good memories will stay near,
To grow with sunshine and with rain,
And help my sorrow disappear,
To make me smile again.

I know such earthly lives are brief,
Perhaps it must be so.
In heaven there is no more grief,
So we must let them go.

But as you take this little one,
I know you will take care
To let the little soul have fun,
Whilst waiting for me there.

THE PERSIAN QUEEN

On velvet cushion, soft and rare,
She sat in majesty supreme
Amongst her many suitors there,
And several bowls of cream.

Long and silky fur to frame
Her enigmatic face,
The ardour of her suitors' flame
Stirs, with her gently moving grace.

Her amber eyes survey the scene,
Pretending they can't see
The passion that is felt so keen,
To challenge feline modesty.

She takes the care we offer her
In her patronising way,
Yet there's independence in her purr,
As she condescends to stay.

That silent charm and dignity,
With paw stretched out to pat
A passing moth so prettily –
She's just someone's pet cat.

YOU NEVER KNOW WHO'S WATCHING

Apart from the major events of our lives, there are also the many
memorably brief moments that for one reason or another stay with us,
and very often we find the reason for this later on. Looked at from the
favourable position of hindsight, we find there was something very

much to our advantage in those isolated encounters, perhaps a lesson to be learnt, probably an opportunity to improve our way of thinking, maybe it was purely an uplifting moment in an otherwise static or even depressing period of our lives, or it could simply be a pointer to help a purely physical condition of the future.

The more we reflect upon these special moments of time, the more we realise that they all have one thing in common – they are not the end product of mere chance. They must indeed be the results of careful planning by someone unseen, perhaps even unacknowledged, who cares about us so much, that with their greater knowledge of us and our future pathways, they can organise these opportunities for us, whilst carefully leaving us our necessary freewill to accept or ignore as we choose.

The patience, skill and sheer kindness of these discarnate spirits who love us so much that they will devote themselves to such organisation, in the full awareness that their efforts may fall on stony ground in spite of all the effort, stuns our minds into disbelief at times. Yet the longer we live, the more we think deeply on such matters, the more we realise – to our great relief – that someone somewhere is watching, waiting, ready to smile or raise a cheer when we respond as they hope we will.

My own memory calls to mind some of these illuminating moments. Some so brief that I cannot even remember the name of the person concerned, perhaps I did not even have the chance to know it. Some other shining brief encounters were through friends and relations of long standing, and although they may have presented me with much of great consequence, still these snippets from our relationship stand out in brilliant isolation – a pole star of the moment. To find these gems amongst the items of one's own treasure chest of memories one must dig deep, their insignificance or crowding out by larger items takes them to the bottom of the box until the light of knowledge shines on them to reveal their true purpose and unfailing worth.

There was the Salvation Army lady at Shoeburyness, where we stayed when I was convalescing from an illness. She introduced us to early wholefood ideas – soaked sultanas on breakfast cereal with plenty of bran, and honey instead of sugar. Such a kindly soul, anxious to help in getting me fit again. We were always influenced by her example and ideas, long before they came ready prepared in packets and at a time when most people thought of such ways as slightly, harmlessly cranky. But our Salvation Army lady had the courage of her convictions, and shared it with us all those years ago, much to our advantage, but I cannot remember her name.

Then there was Mrs. Martin, Headmistress of Wanstead College where I attended school in my early years. She was a vegetarian, and didn't believe in killing anything. This kind and very positive lady used to sit in the garden surrounded by small pots of aromatic contents to keep away unwelcome insects – she literally would not kill a fly! Whatever opinions we may have about this, she made a lasting and noble impression on me, and when the day came for me to be aware of such things and the possibility of vegetarianism, Mrs. Martin whom I had loved and admired as a child, came readily to mind as an example I would like to follow. Somehow her influence from those far off sultry summer days reached out across the years, inspired and encouraged me to make another step forward. Who knows, perhaps it was Mrs. Martin herself who came to me from Spirit with the memory jogging thoughts. Who am I to say it wasn't? Because I really do not know.

The same school brings another clear memory, a senior girl – Joan Hughes – who hit the daily newspaper headlines by qualifying as the youngest solo pilot at fifteen years of age – fame indeed, and we were very proud of her accomplishment – but she also had a lovely voice and her rendering of the First World War song 'Roses of Picardy' at our farewell concert before the school closed down, brought tears to eyes then, and still does whenever I hear that song again, for music has the art of touching the soul at the most unexpected moment. A voice, a piano, a cello perhaps, a nightingale in the still of the night, or a violin. Who pulls the strings of emotions?

My father used to speak of an elderly street violinist who played his music on a London curbside, where passers-by paused in their daily rush to listen. Perhaps others besides my father, knew from that magic street musician, a moment that touched a cord within themselves that sang in harmony with Spirit – briefly and memorably.

Very much earlier in life, there was the wooden tricycle. I must have been about three years old, when my cousin Joan received it as a Christmas present. Around two years my senior, she seemed to have a flair for looking after me, and I well recall her unselfish sharing of this brand new toy. It seemed to me to be the height of achievement to possess such a wonder. The pedals poked out from the front wheel and we could pedal ourselves along in great glee, but I didn't have one, and Joan's willingness to share her prized possession with more than good grace, was an early lesson that has proved a shining example ever since. With my more mature and recent knowledge, I have often thought that perhaps someone was prompting her kindness and my own clear memory of it, why else should such a small incident make such a big impression? Another small kindly act has stayed with me through the years concerning this same cousin – shrimps! We used to often have them for tea on Saturdays. My fingers and patience were too small to shell them, and I recall her own patience as she sat beside me quietly preparing mine before she set about her own. Looking back, it was a commendable demonstration of patient caring for a five year old, a motherly attitude that is not always emulated by adults. We fell down a full flight of stairs together at a very early age – holding hands all the way! Who can say what injuries were avoided by this loving link? I smile even now as I remember looking up at her mother standing at the top of the flight, calling to my own mother "Minnie they've fallen down the stairs". I would think she was frightened to come down and look at us, little did she know that someone unseen was looking after us by linking our hands and reducing the headlong rush to a quiet tumble.

As I recall these mini highlights of very early childhood so clearly, I think they are worth sharing now. It seems we are never too young to learn, as well as never too old, and even humble shrimps can play a part in it!

Years later in my early teens, an opportunity came to me, that I can only regard now as a failure, because I not only allowed it to slip by unused, but to this day I would not know what action to take in similar circumstances.

The incident occurred in a Woolworth store, where counters in those days were long, low, rectangular structures, with a wide slot down the centre for the staff to perambulate, attend to the customers and accept their money. While the assistant served on the opposite side, a middle aged woman on my side was quietly picking up various small articles and whilst examining them, slipping the previous item up her sleeve. I watched in sheer amazement, wondering what to do. I could have called the assistant, or walked quietly to the manager's office and reported the incident, or let the woman know I had seen her, perhaps spoken to her. Maybe that simple act would have jerked her conscience or frightened her to make her think again about her dishonesty. I'll never know, because I did none of these things and merely walked away. Occasionally, as now, my memory will ring this particular rather cracked bell, and it rings a dull note that is somewhat out of tune, because I feel I did not learn from the experience myself, let alone help the misguided person who was stealing. It is always a pity to allow opportunities for progression such as this to pass us by, especially if someone, somewhere has organised them specially for us.

A second and similar opportunity presented me with the same dilemma many years later. Two boys of around ten years of age were the presenters. My reaction was the same as the first occasion. If my friends 'upstairs' are planning a third, I hope my reaction will be better. Maybe Shakespeare put the situation in a metaphoric nutshell, when he causes Hamlet to remark "Conscience doth make cowards of us all". Yes, the next time I believe I shall know the answer, I hope I shall have the courage of my convictions, like my Salvation Army lady of long ago. How fortunate it is for us all that someone somewhere can see the larger picture of our lives and plan to our advantage.

To be on handshaking terms with courage is always an inspiration. It is easy to see and acknowledge the courage of physical bravery – the sudden rescue in acute danger, or the calculated calm of a potentially explosive situation (sometimes quite literally) – but there is another kind of courage, less obvious but in its way equally inspiring, that I have been privileged to meet from time to time.

After our friend Edna had survived a plane crash and later widowed far too early, she picked up the shattered pieces of her life and doggedly rebuilt them into a saga of helping others. Bubbling with cheerful energy in spite of sad reflections behind her own front door, she must have been an upliftment to many. When, many years later, life shattered again in the form of a serious stroke, she produced a different kind of courage to plough her way through the heavy soil of disability and dependence upon others, courage peeping through the curtains of despair. I know her husband helped her from Spirit, because I had proof of his help on a previous occasion. It can be a great upliftment to know that someone 'up there' is watching for such opportunities to help. It can be even greater when we know who it is.

Another example of stoic courage touched my life when my cousin Ivy lost her entire family in less than six months. Her mother, a much loved uncle in residence with them, and her father all passed to Spirit in such a short time. This was closely followed by another uncle passing to Spirit, and another older friend who had known Ivy since she was little more than two years old. She somehow found a strength and courage beyond her own that must have been an example to many.

There are so many unsung heroes in this world of ours, and they have a message for all who care enough to see and understand it, recognising the quality of the moment.

Stoic qualities are revealed in many different ways, and it has been my privilege to share brief moments with many. Those who experience long terminal illness with great calm and courage for instance. Those who are suddenly shattered by terrible physical injury and those whose lives appear to be crumbling beneath the strain of bereavement, family tragedy or the ruin of their livelihood. With others it is a plain dogged determination to achieve that which they believe to be right. I clearly recall the elderly couple of seventy-odd years, who saved their pennies in a teapot on the mantelpiece, doing without things themselves to do so. The reason? it was to pay for a decent burial for the pet dog they loved so much and served them so well. When the time came for that shaggy earthly life to cease at a ripe old age, these two stalwarts walked all of five miles, pushing their pet's body in a box on wheels that the husband had made especially for trips to the vet in latter, failing months of life.

They could ill afford this token of their affection, but they considered it to be a privilege to be able to do it. And as I surveyed this sad, tall upright man and his tiny, quietly grieving wife, I saw in them the shining light of accomplishment. They had done their best, from the birth to death of a dearly loved friend in the only ways they knew. For me it was a brief encounter and a privilege that has survived the test of time.

There was another memorable brief communication many years ago, whilst on holiday. I met a well worn and weathered gardener who asked me if I knew the difference between flowers and weeds. Off hand I couldn't think of one.

"Well" said he – "flowers grow on plants cultivated by man, weeds are flowers that are cultivated by God. Flowers grow with the help of man, weeds grow in spite of him. I'm glad" he added, "that you did not know the difference, it shows that you see them all as the flowers that they are".

I never saw this gentleman of the soil again, but his little homily has remained with me all these years and is well worth recording here, for I see now that his wisdom can also apply to people. Some succeed in life with the artificial aids of man, whilst a few possess a beauty of nature that comes from God. Most of us use a little of both in varying proportions that makes some people nicer to know than others. The beauty of wild flowers blends so perfectly with natural surroundings without the aid of mankind, and they are the root source of all our cultivated garden flowers. Without those weeds we would not have our exotic floral displays. Someone, somewhere, prompted this gardening philosopher to plant a seed of thought in the mind of an unknown adolescent all those years ago, so that one day it could actually go into a book, where many more could see the resultant flower to help them on their way through life, for flowers truly can uplift and make a dull day sparkle, and so can music, kindness, love and laughter.

I will never forget the lovely young nurse at Ham Green Hospital near Bristol, during the early fifties. Her name escapes me, but her face and kindly, gentle nature, and her happy disposition are forever etched upon my memory.

I was a patient there for seven long months, some others were there for longer. Happily, memory seems to dim the darker moments of our lives, whilst brightening the better ones.

When this nurse of happy memory was leaving for pastures new, she said her goodbyes through the hospital radio with the song "You'll Never Walk Alone". I think most of us had a moist eye for one reason or another, but the words of that song gave us all an inner strength and courage, and it has fulfilled the same purpose for me ever since. Her choice of song was an inspiration indeed. Who I wonder, gave her such a valuable thought and who perpetuates that thought through years of events that would appear to have much greater import? Someone 'upstairs' must have been watching then, and it seems – still is.

When we sit in our Rainbow Room for meditation and healing prayer, we light a candle. This began when we used to 'sit' on dark mornings before Ken set off to work – we needed just a glimmer of light and this gentle glow was ideal.

It wasn't long before my mother in Spirit, learned to use the flame to make her presence known to us, and so we have continued the habit. As time went on she would answer questions put by us by the simple expedient of manipulating the flame in certain ways. We have witnessed it climbing to six inches or suddenly letting small sparks fly upwards almost to the ceiling. She can wag the tip of the flame or squash it down until it looks like a fat white snowdrop bulb.

Apart from the usefulness of such a system, we became very much aware of her happy nature around us with the aid of this candle flame, and her sense of fun frequently manifests in this way. Its nice to know she's watching over us and giving us these reminders that she is there.

Fun and laughter are housed down many a Memory Lane, and I well recall the childish giggles when our kite became stuck up a tree, and our laughing attempts to rescue it. And *that* reminds me of more giggles when a golf ball in later years got lodged in a different splendid oak. The giggles turned to laughter when a squirrel popped out of his hole in the trunk and went to inspect this curious 'nut' that had landed on his doorstep. Probably the biggest 'nuts' were on the ground peering helplessly up at the spectacle. Happily he tossed the ball down to us, possibly figuring that the shell was too hard for him to crack – the joke wasn't! and I've smiled at it many times since, for its actually quite a good golfing story to share, that compares favourably with the fisherman's story about the one that got away, though this one happens to be true, and we did get our ball back! I like to think that someone 'Up There' with a nice sense of humour engineered the episode for our delight – and who could prove otherwise?

Sometimes laughter has a healing quality that puts it in a place apart, to shine as a gem in life as long as memory prevails. Shortly after Ken and I had met, at a time when I was merely trying to help him recover from the passing of his first wife Myrtle, we walked along the promenade at Southbourne on a very rough and windy day, with the waves of a high tide crashing spasmodically on to the walkway. Tucking my little dog under my arm and grabbing Ken's hand, I said "Quick we can run between the waves to those little alcoves" – that were just out of reach of the angry sea. We ran and dodged the waves that covered us with spray. We laughed in triumph as we worked our way to a dryer part of the promenade, where even the thunderous crash of the sea could not reach. We were pausing for breath and agiggle at our unsophisticated fun when he said "You are the first person to make me laugh since Myrtle died". I can't remember what I said in reply (if anything at all), but I know the moment became laughter enhanced by my own tears that mingled with the salt of the sea, and looking back, I'm prepared to bet that Myrtle was smiling too, such a lovely lady would be bound to share our friendly and spontaneous laughter, perhaps she even engineered it, because you never know who's watching!

★ ★ ★ ★ ★

DECEMBER GARDEN

The garden seems to sleep beneath the sod,
Unaware of creature, man or God,
But we who know the truth of His own plan,
Bear with all the patience that we can,
The darkest part of yearly life
That bids us now, forgive all strife.
As a robin trills his winter song
To help the frozen days along,
The holly berries sparkle there,
They have no silly grudge to bear.
But man must learn the secret rue
That holly has its prickles too,
In spite of beauteous glossy green
That brightens up our winter scene.

A Christmas rose may dare to breathe
The crispy air — and seek to weave
Pale sunshine into garment rare,
Bright garlands for her sombre hair.
A sheltered snowdrop shyly slips
Into the snowy air, and dips
Her head in needless shame.
She's small, but she's the first that came
To herald a greater floral show,
And means much more than summer's glow.
December's garden sleeps in peace,
Renews her strength — will never cease
To bring the joy of spring again
With wild flowers and leafy lanes.

WELLS OF TRUTH

It is almost Christmas, the annual occasion when fact, legend, myth and mystery join together in a glorious happy mixture to produce the phenomenon of Christmas. From this delectable Christmas pudding it is not easy to sort the fruit of truth from the remaining ingredients, and together they have become so much a part of an accepted whole for so long now that it is actually of little consequence. But it is of interest to realise that the Christmas date itself was borrowed from a pagan belief, the actual date of the birth of Jesus of Nazareth being unknown. It is in fact, a sort of official birthday rather like the official birthday of our Queen instead of her natural one.

Scholars and scientists have attempted to sort many other facts from fiction in this and many other incidents and situations throughout the ages, with a certain amount of success, accompanied by some failure and a fair proportion of uncertainty. It is easy to see how difficult it can be to ascertain and recognise truth, for that, like beauty is often in the eye or ear of the beholder. Different people reporting the same incident, whether it be a family party or an international incident, will frequently give a conflicting view that makes it almost impossible to separate the truth from the false. They are simply seeing the original from different angles.

Truth can sometimes be hidden accidentally because of an inability to adequately express — usually because of a limited knowledge of words or language or an inaptitude with phrasing — most commonly experienced when the speaker is using a language that is foreign to his or her own. The listener thus has to try and glean a meaning from the words spoken and the interpretation may not always relate to the true facts.

* * * * *

In different circumstances altogether, there are situations where truth is deliberately clouded for a variety of reasons, sometimes to spare another person hurt feelings or other emotional pain. More often it is for personal gain in either position or wealth, perhaps both, or sometimes in self defence or protection. The business world and politics on either home or international level are particularly prone to this kind of deceit with eventual disastrous results.

The truth of a situation is frequently hidden by a speaker who is adept at skirting around the main issue with an accumulation of fine sounding words and phrases that hide the truth and are of little or no value to the listener. This little trick of conversation becomes very obvious when someone in authority is questioned about something that he or she cannot, or doesn't wish to answer with complete honesty, and it also occurs when someone has committed a crime or misdemeanour and tried to hide the truth from those who seek to find it.

These are just a few of the ways in which truth is regularly maligned and distorted until it has become an acceptable practice amongst many, who consider they have a right to deceive where they think necessary, and furthermore consider that their listener is the one whose responsibility it is to sort this verbal wheat from the chaff, thus attempting to shift the onus of the results of deception on to someone else — yet another example of the destruction of truth. It is of little consequence to such a person that they are at the time deceiving, and hoping that the results will not catch up with them at a later date.

In times past when the spoken word was rarely recorded in writing, such devious methods of speaking often succeeded where today they would fail because a written record can often be kept. Even more so, the current ability to record the actual voice speaking those words of deception can be a useful deterrent to those who seek to vilify truth. Many public speakers do not always remember as yet this weapon for the protection of truth and fall heavily into the trap it lays. Others who are aware of this sanctuary for truth, refuse to speak if they are to be mechanically recorded, for unlike written recording, they cannot claim inaccuracy on the part of the writer.

One is left to ponder on the reluctance of so many to keep to the truth of a matter. And why should those who write to record or report, be so careless of the true facts that truth cannot shine through their writing. Sometimes it is for personal gain of some kind, or perhaps to protect another person or cause, or often it is a mere ego trip on the part of the writer, who so peppers the work with fine sounding phrases and journalese that the substance of the situation is hidden in the embroidery, and truth suffers in consequence.

These matters are incidents of daily worldly living, and many will feel they are not on the same level of thinking as spiritual truth. But when one stops to consider that life upon this earth is a training ground for a continuous life, it is easy to see how worldly truth is of great importance to us all. For how can we expect to understand the higher spirit truths if we cannot understand and practise more mundane examples of it? While we exaggerate, distort or detract from earthly truth, we cannot hope to glimpse the wonder of spiritual truth, for even if we are granted such a peep into the unknown glory of it, we would not recognise it — it would be completely foreign to our understanding.

In this world, where first we practise to deceive, we can learn to sense the truth of life and action through quiet meditation and appreciation of the natural things around us. If we learn to acknowledge kindness of thought and action in others, and recognise sincerity where it exists in others, we take a great step forward in recognising truth, and by example, learn to use it more effectively ourselves. People are so often afraid of the truth, whereas the truth is really nothing to fear. More often it is the way in which it is delivered to us that we need to fear, and this should be a lesson to ourselves to remember kindness and understanding when we are dealing with truth, as in any other matter of daily living.

Many people find it almost impossible to accept the fact that they will continue to exist after earthly death, still less can they accept that loved ones in the Spirit World can and do contact them, speak to them and help them in their daily lives on earth. Yet these things have been proved many times over. The difficulty lies in the acceptance of the experience of another person. Unless we have the experience ourselves, we feel we cannot be sure, we doubt the truth of another's description of their own enlightenment. Even though we may trust certain other people implicitly in other matters, (we know they would not steal for example), when it comes to matters of the Spirit and other manifestations of the unknown, we are not sure, and wonder if imagination or wishful thinking has played a part. Thus we see how mankind's habitual disregard for the truth has acclimatised us all to the possibility of deceit, and so in sheer self protection our minds are schooled to disbelieve, depriving us of the joys of truth, of honesty of thought and action, of recognition of sincerity in others. The loss of these hinders our own progress towards those self same attributes.

Too much pain and sorrow, suspicion and despair are generated by mankind's disregard for truth. Just one person deviating from truth can affect thousands or more, and this can be a frightening thought when you come to consider it fully. It is only too obvious that no individual can persuade the rest of humanity to change course on such a fundamental attitude, but it is worth bearing in mind the fact that all true religions are based upon the need for truth, in spite of the varying interpretations inserted by leaders of those religions through the ages. For truth is still a root prerequisite, and as there are so many religious groups, sects and beliefs, it clearly involves many millions of people. If at least some of those people would begin a campaign for real truth in the everyday workings of earthly life, many others would be alerted to the truth of their appeal, and by adding to it themselves, enhance that truth and in their turn add to the sum total of the whole. It would not take too long for honesty of thought and action to become as acceptable as the opposite is accepted at the present time.

All life and action is so much happier, less complicated, and more rewarding when we adhere to truth. Most of us know the difference between truth and deceit, how much easier many consciences would be if the path of truth were followed, for truth begets truth, whilst deceit of any kind invariably begets further deceit. If a soul has nothing to hide from its fellow man, then life and thinking are simplified, the door is opened to trust and love of every kind, with peace in the world as the inevitable star prize.

Seek and ye shall find, the Bible tells us, yet how few of us really seek for truth. Perhaps we fear what we may find, but those who have embarked upon this endeavour have shown many times over how peace of mind can be a just reward, bringing with it a joy of living they had not known existed. The truth of the knowledge of continued life after so-called death, can inspire a new outlook of hope and happiness such as most people can only dream of. This should not be, and certainly need not be. If someone communicates with you via a telephone, you do not normally question who they are once they have made themselves known to you. Apart from an occasional and rare joker, or someone of ill intent, you accept that they are not only there on the other end of the line, but accept that they are in fact who they say they are. Yet if that same person had passed from this life to the next and wished to communicate, and succeeded — many would doubt their authenticity, some would openly scorn. How sad they would be on the other end of your telephone line if you doubted the truth of their words and identity. How sad too they must be if we choose to ignore or denounce them when they contact us from the World of Spirit. If only we learned to recognise and practice truth such sadness need not be.

In the depth of the soul of each one of us, is the knowledge of God, the truth of eternal life and love, we can see it and hear it, be aware of it in the existence of planets, the universe, the perfect working of these and all other things of nature, the balance and the beauty that somehow survives all that mankind does to it.

The truth of these things is there for all to see and accept. Our own individual desire for truth and our own efforts to draw the pure water from the Well of Truth within us, will open our eyes to the even greater truths of Spirit — if we choose to let it be so. It is our own responsibility to ourselves that opens the door, not only to our own joyful progression, but also towards the eventual greater harmony of the world.

A PLACE AND TASK FOR HUMOUR

December, with its Christmas time, is a happy part of the year. For Christians it has a particular meaning, and this demonstrates the effectiveness of the power of thought, because their Christmas joy extends to all around them, the power of their thoughts bringing a happy lightness of spirit to others, no matter what their religion may be. It also demonstrates the futility of allowing differences of opinion on that subject to affect our lives in any detrimental way. It can spoil friendships, break up families and even cause wars.

Tolerance in religion would overcome so many difficulties, for tolerance, kindness and humour are universal languages that have no ordinary barriers, but can bind friendships, families and nations towards happiness and peace.

Kindly humour that springs a twinkle in the eyes and a relaxing of the muscles, not only creates a happy understanding between people, but also promotes a harmony within those people. It physically and mentally helps everyone concerned, and how could anyone quarrel with someone who has just shared their gentle joke?

The importance of humour cannot be overestimated. The importance of its nature must also be realised if it is to be of any value at all. Sarcastic wit that hurts and crushes is not even related to humour. It is merely a device to inflate the speaker's ego, whilst trying to demean another person — a weapon of spite and sharp barbs that tears the mind and emotions of both sender and recipient. Yet kindly wit can heal and lift to untold heights. Its light can brighten any pathway no matter how dark it may seem, for this is the light that has its source in a happy motivation — this is the light that can shine for all, no matter who or where they are, or what their beliefs or understanding may be. No better way has ever been found of spreading happiness.

The following poem was received for our friend Ron, to enclose with a modest fishing tackle Christmas gift and give him a smile as a Christmas Card.

A FISHY TALE (Tail?)

A little fish was hiding there,
In an old grandfather's chair,
When a fishy hook he spied –
How his eye did open wide!
Did someone think he ever would
Grab it — even if he could?

With wriggly worms down in the sand,
Nymphs and beetles all at hand,
Who would bite a silly hook,
Or even take a second look —
At something dangled there by man,
I know he'd catch me if he can.

But wait I think that's Ron up there,
Probably just sat in prayer,
Hoping I will take his baits,
While he sits and meditates,
It seems a shame to disappoint,
And throw his day all out of joint.

Besides, he's very nice is Ron,
Patience should be rewarded soon,
Then life for him will nothing lack,
Because I know he'll toss me back
Into the waters that I love —
Happy Christmas Ron above.

He'll never catch me dozing on,
I'd better help give him a run
Of better luck for Christmas time,
I'll tweak the hook to give a sign,
A Christmas present for a day,
And be the one that got away!

And Ron can tell the tale all year,
How a giant fish filled him with fear,
Lashing, towing, thrashing foam,
Never would get this one home.
It's fun to play a fisherman,
And give him all the sport you can.

No-one knows but little me,
How very easy it would be —
To look and laugh and swim away,
To live again another day.
And Ron will help me sing my song —
'Cos I am just three inches long!

WIDER THOUGHTS OF CHRISTMAS

Christmas means different things to different people, for although it has a very specific meaning to all true Christians of the world, its impact is far greater.

Initially a pagan celebration, then borrowed to commemorate the birth of Christianity, Christmas made a happy contribution in uniting different beliefs right from its very beginning. The fact that, along with other religions, Christianity later shared the responsibility of creating disharmony and even wars, is not the fault of Christianity itself, but the weaknesses of the people of knowledge and power at varying times in the history of mankind.

Through all the years of love and unity, turmoil, division and pain, Christmas survives as a symbol of peace and love that infiltrates the lives of Christians and non-Christians the world over. It is the time of year when thoughts of giving outweigh thoughts of receiving, and people who have lost touch with one another for twelve whole months, again contact friends and relations and renew the ties that bind memories and emotions.

Unkind thoughts and actions that permeate all other days, are often laid aside at Christmas. Somehow, the love that has built up around it through the years, manages not only to survive the man-made ravages of time, but grows and spreads its wings and flies to all corners of the world. It is a classic example of the power of thought.

Man can try to denigrate it, capitalise on it, make it an excuse for all manner of excesses, but still Christmas reigns supreme in its role of promoting goodwill and kindliness. Whatever our religious belief may be, it is certain that we will all be touched by Christmas in some way or other, and it is an encouraging thought that in this materialistic world, Christmas can still be so instrumental in bringing together so many who would otherwise remain apart — can still promote goodwill and kindliness, and keep alive a love of humanity that otherwise might die.

Those who do not adhere to Christian beliefs, may feel that they cannot celebrate Christmas with honesty of thought. But this must surely be a narrow point of view. With wider thinking, we can recognise that anything which can promote kindly thought and action is worthy of acceptance for its own sake. Labels often seem to narrow uses, and in the case of Christmas, it would be foolish indeed to discard such a valuable source of goodwill, merely because of the label of its origin. After all, we have already noted that this time of celebration is itself sharing the occasion with other beliefs, and demonstrating the value of tolerance and acceptance.

It may well be that these were not the motives of those who initiated this amalgamation, and indeed, history suggests that the reasons at the beginning were much more self-centred. But this is of little consequence to us today. The results of those early actions are of much greater import. Some of the results leave much to be desired, but others are great bounty, and it is for us to sort the wheat from the chaff and reap a valuable harvest. The love, goodwill, and emphasis on peace at Christmas time, is the legacy we have inherited, and it is the failure of mankind to use that inheritance to full advantage, that gives us such cause for sorrow.

If all that is good in this world were shared and accepted as readily as Christmas time, what a wonderful place it would be in which to live. Yet each one of us can further the spirit of Christmas, merely by extending the loving tolerance and kindly thoughts towards others the whole year round. Forgiving, understanding, throwing away the bonds of jealousy and mistrust, simply loving others in the widest meaning. Such thoughts can spread so wide, can smooth so many pathways, link the minds of friends, heal old wounds.

As each kind thought wings its way from one soul to another, it promotes another kindly thought and deed — just like a Christmas present.

A MESSAGE OF CHRISTMAS

The Christmas message gleams with love,
 For all the world to see,
When hope will shine like stars above,
 That all men may be free.

The Christmas message links true friends,
 Though many a mile apart,
And to a saddened world it lends
 Kind thoughts to cheer the heart.

For when such thoughts fly round the world,
 They sing in harmony,
The flag of truth and peace unfurled
 Uniting pure sincerity.

Thus the friendship love spreads wide,
 It speaks of hope and courage.
When truth and faith walk side by side,
 They bring the Christmas message.

CANDLE POWER

What a splendid thing is a candle, what great versatility it has displayed
throughout the years of its existence, this mere stick of wax and cotton.
 Nowadays, candles come in many colours and fancy shapes, and

take their place as ornaments upon the mantleshelf, never to be lit and act out their true function, lest they melt and spoil their beauty, or the giver be offended that their gift is destroyed by the very function of its nature.

This should surely never be, this travesty of a noble article that has given such splendid service to mankind, a service which mankind himself could rightly envy. For what greater service could there be than to light the world, brighten dark corners of fear, and comfort the lonely. The humble candle succeeds where mankind so often fails.

Shakespearian writings express the achievement superbly – "How far that little candle throws his beams, so shines a good deed in a naughty world."

Whoever first made a candle, could have had little idea of its worth, or its future. History tells us of its use many hundreds of years ago, and it is a sobering thought, that as the Romans lit their way amongst the columns and portals of their times, so we today can still use the simple candle to light our own way when modern expertise fails.

The many uses of the candle must defy all opposition in the competition for variety of use. Think of the early miners as they crept their way underground, with only a candle to guide them. Compare this action with that of the young child making his way to bed — up there beyond the stairs, in the dark cold world of ancient bedrooms. In each action, so many miles apart, the candle was a lifeline to coherent thought and action.

People have used candles as part of their worship to their particular God all through the ages. For churches have made good use of candles, to light their lofty buildings, or bring together prayerful thought amongst their congregations. And at the other end of this particular scale, the black witches of yore, used candles in their black magic and darkly intended spells. Would that they had used such a beautiful object to better purpose.

Others through the ages have seen fit to use the candle for foul purpose, the licking of the flame upon flesh as a means of torture, was a simple way of trying to extract confessions, either true or false. Even some religious bodies can rightly bow their heads in shame for this. It is a happier thought that this is not the fault of the candle, but the diabolical use to which man has put it from time to time.

How many good things and true, have been misused by man in the same way. Mankind must be the only occupier of this earth that can turn some good thing or action to improper use and thereby seek to destroy its very nature. Yet man considers himself the superiors of earth's inhabitants, whilst a mere candle can prove this impression of himself to be false. Ah, the power of the simple candle.

Ladies in their crinolines, once sat with silk or satin folding gracefully around shy, shapely legs, nimble fingers effecting fine embroidery. Beside them in a candlestick of gold or silver, stood the humble candle, without whose light their task could not be accomplished.

Not too far away perhaps, another exponent of this noble art of needle and thread, would be sitting on her hard and well worn wooden seat, stitching together some garment that her child would need tomorrow, her stiff dark skirts of hessian or closely woven wool, sweeping the floor around her chair, collecting todays fluff and yesterdays mud. Beside her stood the pottery or wooden holder, or perhaps if not too poor, one made of brass or iron from the forge down the road, proudly supporting the light of a candle, that this humble soul too could see the way to sew. The vessel might be different in both looks and value, but the light thus supported would be the same, and the difference in the candlestick would matter not one jot.

Amongst the millions of good and kindly deeds performed each day, amounting to a veritable mountain of goodness will be the vast variety of human vessels who hold each good deed of light to illuminate the way for those in need. Some will be rich, some will be poor, some richly clothed, others draped in muddy tatters, and millions more be dressed according to their station in life and inclination, somewhere between the two. Their light will shine upon this naughty world in imitation and purity of the candles' flame, no value will be added to the deed, or yet subtracted from it, because of position or appearance of the giver.

Even the sparse warmth of the candle's flame has comforted many a frozen hand, and through that hand, extended comfort to the soul.

Where now the motor car speeds its deadly way, with straight beams of light to pierce the gloom in front, there once were rattling iron bound wheels, with horses straining at the traces, and but a candle in a carriage lamp. This lamp did not beam out to infiltrate the darkness, but more to bob and curtsey over every rut and hole, and tell of its approach to those who came the other way. Even lighthouses in the past were lit with candles, the mirrored light warning seafarers of dangers on the rocks. Yet as they warned, these candles stretched a welcome too, that many a sailor must have been relieved to see.

Every welcoming hand stretched out is but a candlelight for an enlightened soul to see. And those who brush aside this gentle glow, and say, "It is not bright enough for me", will miss the loving warmth of the candles well tried flame, and prefer the garish illumination that someone else can douse with one flick of a switch, or harsh unkindly word.

Children have played and laughed, shrieking with delight at the sight of candles on a Christmas tree. The flickering light turns tinsel into diamonds and holly berries into rubies of such size, to make any child gasp. Any yet the child who is tired, sick or lonely, takes comfort, even hope from a candle's warming flame. The soft light soothes, and brings its friend, the welcome sleep, that cures, replenishes and strengthens for another day. Vast fortunes are spent for such gifts as these, and yet the humble candle gives for modest pence, the same result.

And if at times, the shadows cast by candlelight, should bring a fear, and nerves are taut with wild uncertainty, 'tis not the fault of the candle, but merely the dark imaginings of the one who thinks he sees. For others see not fear, but jolly shapes and friendly fairies dancing on the wall. The candle shows you what you wish to see. Throughout your life your freewill gives the right for you to interpret as you will, for good or ill, and this interpretation is exactly what you see.

Candles have shed their light in shops and cells, or wooden huts or castles. Their light has glowed in dining rooms, and kitchens where cooks have brought forth great culinary masterpieces, with the aid of the light of a candle. Pictures have been painted and barbers snipped off hair and beards, with no more aid than scissors and a candle. Babies have been born, and those who have lived their earthly span, have gratefully gone on to better things, their way lit merely by a candle.

Plants in greenhouses have been spared the ravages of frost, and water stopped from freezing, simply by our friend the candle. Lovers have proposed in romantic candlelight, and carol singers warbled at front doors with candles in their jars. Candles carry out their tasks equally well, whether they are ensconced in elaborate candelabra in some great noble hall, or stuck in ungainly fashion, on a saucer that this morning fed the cat with milk.

If people could but see, that like the candle, it is their tasks in life that they must well perform, and care not about the bric-a-brac of the numerous candleholders in their lives. Then this world would be a happier place in which to live, a place where true values would hold sway, brightened by a giant flame of love.

"Candle Power" was a piece of inspirational writing delivered at great speed, much faster than I would normally write. It was followed by this poem which was started in September 1987. The incomplete piece was put away and virtually forgotten until some more verses arrived in December, and we recalled the earlier communication and found they fitted together perfectly.

Candles

How still the candle flame can stand –
Erect and noble in its stance –
To light the world around its flame,
To show the way of peace at last.

One candle may not light the world,
Yet reaching out its golden rays,
The brightness yet is still untold,
But turns the darkness into days.

Many candles shining bright,
Would reach around our darkened world,
Gleaming through the darkest night –
Every good deed now unfurled.

And so each soul could shine as these –
Linking with another soul –
To spread the thought of kindly deeds,
And so – all Spirit love unfold.

And thus God's love remains supreme
In comfort, like the candle's glow.
And we can help create the team
Of shining peace that makes it so.

A POSTSCRIPT

I hope you have enjoyed sharing some of my memories – a pot-pourri of time and circumstances that individually are merely bits and pieces of a very ordinary life, but together make a bowl of colour and perfume that stays the test of time to give renewed moments of delight every now and then.

If my readers have found pleasure for themselves somewhere in this bowl of memories and spiritual communications, perhaps a smile, maybe the dawn of a new and happy thought, then I am well content. If a few have found some help or comfort in addition, then the effort of collecting and presenting the material has been worth while.

To end, I offer you a poem that seems to sum up the message of the bells that I have tried to give, and by happy chance the title is also the name of our own home, which seems to me to be another full circle, which this time actually enfolds a soul with earthly life still in the making. All blessings to you as your own pathways unfold.

★ ★ ★ ★ ★

TRANQUILLITY

The light of God is the love of peace,
For all mankind to see,
The peace of God will never cease
To bring tranquillity.

Oh peace that comes from the depth of mind,
  The tranquil moments of our lives,
When all our thoughts are gently kind,
  Contentment blooms as gentle sighs.

The memory slips with easy stride,
  Through many a passing door,
And music tugs where thoughts abide,
  To stay for evermore.

For the love of God is a peaceful scene,
  Of memory drifting through the words
Of love, and all that would have been
  Bright haloes in His other world.

No fear, no anxious moments dwell
  Where love and faith in God prevails,
Or memory spins to ring the bells,
  As Tranquillity sets sail.

The Encircling Year

I N D E X